Loving the Stranger

Studies in Adolescence,
Empathy and the Human Heart

LOVING THE STRANGER

STUDIES IN ADOLESCENCE, EMPATHY AND THE HUMAN HEART

Dr Lotte Sahlmann
Dr Thomas J. Weihs
Anke Weihs
Birgit Hansen
Angelika Monteux
Michael Schmundt
Michael Luxford

Compiled and edited by
Michael Luxford

Camphill Books

1st Edition 2000

Published by TWT Publications Ltd
on behalf of
The Camphill Movement

© 2000 Camphill Youth Guidance Faculty

British Library CIP Data
A catalogue record of this book is available from the British Library

ISBN 1 897839 18 9

*This publication has been assisted by the
Camphill Foundation in the British Isles*

Acknowledgements

Compiling this book would not have been possible without the ongoing research work that has been carried out since at least 1979 by many individuals and groups within the Camphill Movement.

It was as a result of their involvement in this activity that the editor was able to put together this volume and present his own thoughts which give the book its title. For this reason he wishes to express his gratitude to those who have worked, and continue to work, out of this impulse of Youth Guidance.

Thanks are especially due to Andrew Shackleton of Asgard Publishing Services for his involvement and the many helpful comments made during the editorial process.

Special thanks also to Ninetta Sombart for allowing the use of her painting *The Raising of Lazarus: the Rich Young Man* as an image for the book cover; also to the Henry Moore Foundation for permission to publish a photograph of the sculpture *Mother and Child* by Henry Moore, and to Friedwart Bock for his photograph of the Chapel in Camphill Hall, Aberdeen.

Contents

'O, have faith, my heart!
O, have faith.
Nothing shall you lose,
Yours is, your very own,
Everything you experience,
All your suffering is yours!
'You will rise again,
Yes! Rise again,
My heart,
After a short sleep!'

Thus I sang, bearing my heart in my breast as though it were the most precious thing on earth — which indeed it is — for faith lives in the heart like the full-throated song of the birds that pours forth into all the world.

[From *A Christmas Story* by Karl König. Camphill Press 1995]

Introduction

Loving the Stranger is an attempt to create a holistic research document in the field of Youth Guidance, intended primarily for those who have an interest in the situation and experiences of young people of today. However, it is not meant to be all-encompassing. It adopts a particular approach to the subject that has mainly to do with the fundamental change which takes place in the human heart at this vital stage in human development.

This book's approach can be described as holistic in that it involves making observations and gaining insights from day-to-day involvement with young people and expanding these to include thoughts and impressions resulting either from our own reflection and questioning or from the study of significant researchers in the field such as Rudolf Steiner, R. D. Laing and Erik Erikson.

In particular, use is made of what is presented by Anthroposophy, by which is meant the development of our consciousness of our humanity through understanding, knowledge and an all-round appreciation of human existence and the world as they appear in sensible as well as spiritual dimensions.*

As a starting point you will find here an explanation of certain characteristics of the human heart and what takes place in and around it, and in relation to it, as puberty sets in within child development. This time of life opens the door to adolescence and the phase of youth experience. It is a crucial time of transition, leading the individual out of childhood into the beginnings of adult life.

In the first two chapters Dr Lotte Sahlmann introduces aspects of her lifelong research, based on Rudolf Steiner's lecture on the human

---

* A further elaboration of the meaning of anthroposophy etc. is given in the opening remarks of: Rudolf Steiner. *Anthroposophy — A Fragment.* Anthroposophical Press, 1996.

heart given in 1922. The first two chapters are devoted to describing his indications so that we can relate to them or picture them for ourselves.

In the third chapter, by way of contrast to Dr Sahlmann's medical background, Birgit Hansen looks at the same phenomena in relation to the human heart, but from the viewpoint of the teacher. She includes remarks by her pupils and uses examples from her experience in education, and particularly curative education.* It is central to her contribution that she questions the normally held idea that the heart is a pump.

New ways of understanding the heart, beyond its function as a bodily organ, are being discovered. Witness two books on the phenomena which can occur following heart transplants. These are clearly described, verifiable accounts of patients who after transplant surgery found themselves experiencing characteristics in themselves which had once belonged to the donor. Such accounts can be found in Claire Sylvia's *A Change of Heart* and Paul Pearsall's *The Heart's Code* (both books are listed under Further Reading at the end of this book).

In the chapters that follow, having entered by this doorway of the heart and its spiritual and physical dimensions, we are encouraged to examine the heart from the point of view of the development of empathy. This is not to say the empathy has its foundations solely in the heart. This is not the case, as the organ we are beginning to acquire, and which enables us to experience the world and others empathetically, has primarily to do with the development of our senses.† But the capacity of empathy can be seen as lying between the cognitive pole of the head and the focus of will activity, which expresses itself via our limbs and metabolic system. Empathy reaches out into the world and returns to itself continuously in rhythmic sequence, and here we find a connection between empathy and the formation and functioning of the heart and its peripheral system.

The late authors of the next two chapters on empathy, Dr Thomas Weihs and Anke Weihs, were founder members of the Camphill Movement.‡ During their lifetimes they were engaged in the medical,

---

* For a description of the nature of curative education, see: Michael Luxford. *Children with Special Needs*. Floris Books, 1994.
† This subject is elaborated in the books listed under 'Empathy' in the Further Reading section at the end of this book.

psychiatric and therapeutic fields, and they possessed a lifelong interest in the needs of young people, particularly those with behavioural and social difficulties. Angelika Monteux's more recent contribution in the subsequent chapter creates a link to present-day manifestations of empathy.

The following four chapters have to do with some of the disturbances and potential pathologies associated with the adolescent phase of life. The aetiologies of psychosis, schizophrenia, anorexia nervosa and so-called maladjusted behaviour are described, and ways of extending help and healing are indicated.

The penultimate chapter is based on Michael Schmundt's notes from a conference on social maladjustment in children and young people, and will be of interest to those who are concerned about the behaviour of some young people. He also describes the problems caused by an over-academic approach to learning, particularly among young children. Today this happens at the expense of other equally valid and valuable capacities which should be nurtured but are nowadays often neglected. We should not see the difficulties faced by young people as simply being of their own making, or even as being due to some vague sociological or environmental cause. They may be related to apparently wholesome trends in primary education and child care which only show their effect years later in what can be described as maladjusted or disturbed behaviour in young adults.

The final chapter, which lends its name to the book — *Loving the Stranger* — follows up yet a further insight provided by Rudolf Steiner with regard to young people and their development. If the first part of the book is to do with the human heart, and the second to do with the relationship between the processes of sympathy and antipathy as they work in us, then the third is to do with the realisation that karma and reincarnation can to some extent become tangible to our experience and can be seen as being related to life, especially at certain crucial transitional points in human development — in this case in the time of

---

‡ The Camphill Movement began in 1940 in Aberdeen, Scotland, working with children, young people and adults with special needs. It has since become a world-wide movement active in 20 countries, with the aim of forming healing, therapeutic communities in urban or rural settings that address a wide range of needs, including those of the land. Karl König's history of the Movement is listed among the references at the end of the book.

youth. This chapter also places particular emphasis on the significance of the relationship between what we carry out in daily life, in our activities, and what results from these at night when we go to sleep. It also relates this search to the Christian path, which is to do with the attainment of selfless love and the forces of resurrection that exist beyond illness, suffering, sleep and death.

In a way this chapter needs to be approached as much through our heart forces as through our power of understanding. If we look back over humanity's development we can recognise without too much difficulty or dispute two distinct phases: the phase of mythological thinking or conception, followed by what might crudely be called the phase of the intellect. (We can recognise this in the qualitative difference between the means of expression found in Homer, for instance, and what is present in the writings of Aristotle.) We can also say that earlier forms of conception (thought life) were artistic in character — poetic — whilst what came later became a basis for a scientific methodology.

This approach is linked to a further step which we as modern people need to take with regard to our life of thinking: to move from our earlier stage of thought life, through the relatively recent phase of intellectually gained conceptions, into imaginative ideation and reflective image-forming as a conscious activity. These steps can be summarised as follows:

Mythological thinking	Intellectual development	Imaginative ideation
(past)	*(present)*	*(future)*

Therefore, the approach to Youth Guidance found here is not another attempt to develop sociological, psychological, emotional or behavioural insights with regard to the young person. There is a tremendous amount of literature already on these subjects. It is an attempt to enter the world of *the stranger* — the personality who begins to emerge as a young person at the end of childhood. The way to do this, the doorway, is via a study of the human heart and the changes it undergoes during puberty.

The three main themes considered in this book can be summarised as follows:

1 The changes taking place in the heart organism at the time of puberty.

2 Understanding the working of sympathy and antipathy in the human soul and the development of empathy.

3 Recognising karma and reincarnation as factors which influence the biographies of individuals, and particularly at certain nodal points.

It is to be hoped that this book will strengthen awareness for what has already grown out of the practice of Youth Guidance, while also making apparent to us what is at stake in the lives of young people today, who are often subjected to so much excitement, novelty and distraction, most of which in the end does little justice to their individual purposes, which are to bring new spiritual, social and creative impulses into a world which always tends towards ageing and has time and again to be renewed and refreshed by the forces of youth.

Michael Luxford
1999

Adolescence and the human heart

Youth Guidance Conference, Blairdrummond, Scotland, 7 November 1981

Adolescence is a period when young people are particularly liable to emotional stress. Indeed, every adolescent will at some stage experience a tremendous sense of bewilderment and a burning need to find answers to their questions. But in order to understand the problems associated with adolescence — the third seven-year period of life* — we shall first need to reappraise some of the spiritual and physiological processes that take place within the heart over this period.

In order to do this, it is of primary importance for us to develop, through our warmth of heart as well as our intellectual understanding, an open-minded attitude towards young people — for without this we will never achieve the necessary empathy for their situation. Such an attitude may often provide the only security in what for them can seem to be a crumbling world. We need to develop and communicate the vital warmth that they have so much need of — a challenge that will become all the more real to us as we reconsider the various transformations that take place within the heart organisation during adolescence.

The background

As far as we know, Rudolf Steiner dealt with this particular aspect of the change in the human heart only once — in 1922[1] — leaving us with the task of analysing his comments and evaluating their significance. In many of his lectures, especially those to teachers, Steiner spoke about

---

* Human life can be considered from the point of view of the rhythmic processes of development. These are most marked in childhood, which can be said to show three distinct phases: early childhood (0–7 years), the time of creative play and building of the body; schoolchild (7–14 years), a gradual freeing from the family and the beginning of education; and adolescence (14–21 years), during which time, beginning with puberty, a marked change takes place. The ages are approximate, especially today, but do indicate a rhythmic development that continues throughout human life.

the birth of the *etheric* body, which is unique to each of us and replaces the borrowed inherited forces that have determined our life up until then.* In this time of early childhood, these etheric forces mould and form our organs, making them our own, but the human heart is the one organ in the body that behaves differently, waiting another seven years before it discards the worn-out inherited garment and clothes itself with its own etheric structure.

Around the time of conception, we form our etheric body from the universal world ether. At this moment the whole cosmic potential of life is available to us, subject to our past experiences and behaviour. This begins to work in us, and the associated forces, imprinted with cosmic powers, gradually radiate their strength into our physical structure, until by the age of seven they have replaced the inherited life forces. From then on the etheric body changes, but concentrates some of its forces on the place where the physical heart lies, until by the time of puberty a new etheric organ has been formed.

In a similar way, although for totally different reasons, our soul forces unite with our physical organs by the age of puberty. These soul forces carry with them our past karma: our destiny insofar as it has become manifest between our previous death and our present birth. It is thus in the heart of each individual that destiny meets with our cosmic etheric powers, forging an intimate bond between the earthly soul life of man and the cosmic powers of the universe.

Following these spiritual and physiological events, the totality of our astral body† is then ready to receive the imprint of all that we do, say or achieve throughout life. Everything and anything that happens in the world through our own deliberate action — whether good or bad, courageous or foolish — is imprinted into the astral body, and from there it will eventually permeate the newly formed astral heart. It is out

---

* The etheric body is the name given to the body of forces which provide the living element within the human being. These forces are also present in the natural world and are the bearers, not only of life, but of rhythm and memory.

† The astral body is overtly active in animals and humans. It gives us the faculties of movement, sensory experience, instinctive action, and feelings of sympathy or antipathy (explained in a later footnote). These forces become dissociated from us during sleep, and return when we awaken. They endow animals and humans with a certain consciousness of the world around, but not with self-awareness, morality, language or thought, which only the higher organisation of the human ego can engender.

of this process that our future karma begins to form itself, and it will be retained within our organism until we die, at which stage these imprints are passed on to the cosmic powers.

The years around and after puberty are therefore tremendously decisive, and consequently full of tension. The new destiny meets the old one — battling and wrestling with all the things from the past that have to be transformed, redeemed and developed further. The human heart is at the centre of this struggle, its task being to listen, harmonise and transform what takes place in life. This is a battle that must be fought within every human being, whatever their constitution might be.

Childhood has so far been dominated by events experienced at a deeply subconscious level, but from now on the adolescent becomes consciously aware of the drama and struggle going on within him. He is plagued by deep questions and searching existential doubts as to the meaning and aims of life. He must wrestle with questions of birth and death, childhood and adulthood, good and evil, family and country — and must accept or reject them just as the burdens of his destiny start to impinge increasingly on his consciousness.

This third seven-year period of life stands mainly under the zodiacal sign of Cancer — the sign of the crab — symbolising a stage when our past existence is virtually separated from all that the future might have in store. Into this gulf the ego descends ever more deeply as we struggle to come to terms with what we are, what we look like, our family and circumstances. We must first cross this chasm, represented in ♋ (the zodiacal sign for Cancer), before we can start on our future path. For only then are we capable of dealing with ourselves at a more conscious level. It may take several years before our ego finds itself safely anchored in the harbour, sheltered at last from all this turbulence — a period that can be traumatic for anyone, regardless of whether they have some learning difficulty or not.

Practical considerations: learning difficulties

Adolescence is the time when the birth of the intellect takes place* and

---

* The birth of the astral body, beginning at puberty, signifies increasingly conscious soul experiences, revealed in three predominant manifestations: thinking, feeling and willing. The growth of intellectual capacities, the emergence of a strong emotional life, and the increased intentionality, point to its occurrence and to its threefold character.

our threefold soul existence begins to mature. Consequently, it is precisely at this time when young people in need of soul care will tend to falter in their development. Their will-forces may sometimes overpower them, while their emotional life may be beset by subconscious drives. In other young people it may be the power of feeling which begins to dominate, so that they experience the world in a state of pure sympathy or antipathy* — neither of which gives them any degree of inner freedom.

The question therefore arises as to how educators and parents can help stimulate and foster the development of these young people through this difficult and decisive stage in their lives. There are three main strategies that can be employed:

1 All youngsters, even those who need a good amount of special soul care, are subject to bewilderment and doubt throughout these years. Such emotions are healthy and, if carefully guided and directed, will lead to the necessary steps of development. They may be a first step towards a certain awakening of the ego, a greater realisation of potentials or weaknesses, and a first opening towards an acceptance of one's destiny — past as well as future. Furthermore, this realisation may lead to a more conscious questioning of oneself, one's aims and motivations, against a background of often very complicated life situations. Regular talks, individually as well as in group settings, are indispensable, providing a kind of image of a developing humanity which is visible in the script of history and the growth of social conscience. The more we can create images based on the biographies of certain significant personalities, the better we may succeed in engendering and strengthening the forces of morality and compassion. Though deprived to a large measure of intellectual capacity, the forces of the heart can still grow and expand, and through their response help to lead the ego into the future. During this latter

---

* The terms *sympathy* and *antipathy* are used here in an unusual way — not in the customary moral sense, but in the sense of *involvement* and *non-involvement*. At the pole of the *will* (sympathy) we are continuously involved with the world and with other human beings. At the pole of *consciousness* (antipathy) we are able to think and form concepts, but cannot be involved or we would not be able to be conscious. These concepts are later considered further by Michael Schmundt in (*see page 79 ff*).

time of adolescence, there may be some doubt as to whether a school setting is still right, and a much more flexible approach to learning may have to be devised.

2 Occupation with the three kingdoms of nature (mineral, plant, animal), using a simplified phenomenological approach, stressing metamorphosis and training pure observation, will help to awaken the qualities of compassion and awe.

3 A third step towards full maturation is the right approach to questioning. The figure of Parzival* now becomes relevant. No matter what level of intellect a young person shows, he or she should always be challenged to ask, to doubt, and not only to accept. The path to inner freedom leads through the forest of doubt, and it is interest in the world, wanting to know, wishing to succeed, which are the instruments that will make the journey worthwhile and possible. It is the task of educators, parents and others to kindle in the growing youngster the flame of his or her individuality, and to do this requires our moral fantasy, empathy and enthusiasm.

In addition to the three tasks mentioned above, the acquisition of skills and a working morale will play a decisive part. To work in socially and economically real ways belongs to the dignity of every human being, enhances his image of himself, but also creates future destiny as these deeds begin to inscribe themselves into the astral heart.

In his lectures on the *Karma of Vocation*[2] Rudolf Steiner points to the significance for the future of manual and other work. He says that even mechanical and repetitive work is connected with the forming of future karma, and that various philosophic, cultural and artistic activities, as well as craft work, can fulfil past destiny if they are carried out with satisfaction and joy.

These words of Rudolf Steiner from 1916 have to be understood, and their significance introduced into our practical work with young people. To enter into their implications requires much intensive study and discussion, but to take up this theme is to be concerned with the

---

* Parzival, in the story told by the poet Wolfram von Eschenbach, is the mediaeval knightly figure who has to endure doubt, loneliness and the encounter with his own frailty, on the way to the Grail Castle and becoming its king.

importance of economic life, the future and the furtherance of the threefold social organism,* as well as the future karma of our young people.

Conclusion

We started with a description of the supersensible changes taking place in the human heart from puberty onwards. Into this virgin organ we have to bring harmonising influences during the years of adolescence. Whatever we inscribe into this central organ will have to stand up to the highest spiritual judgement linking to future destiny.

The qualities of awe and wonder, compassion, conscience and morality, are the qualities of the human heart. These qualities meet with all the deeds inscribed by our work, skills, play and speaking to form out the karma of a future life on earth.

---

* The threefold social organism describes social life according to three definable aspects: a cultural, artistic and spiritual sphere; a legal and political sphere; and an economic, productive realm. For the social organism to be healthy, these aspects need to be recognised in their characteristics and requirements, and principally in their application to freedom, democracy and the meeting of needs.

Further notes on the human
heart during adolescence

Youth Guidance Course, Pennine Camphill Community, 27 February 1998

The structure of human heart has been known to anatomists and physiologists ever since the first beginnings of scientific research. Throughout that time it has been considered to be a pump. It is found in the centre of the human body, slightly to the left and just above the diaphragm, and leans forward at an angle of about 23 degrees. Its position alone indicates a cosmic relationship to the earth, which begs the question as to whether the heart is indeed a pump. A good many people say that this is not so for some of the following reasons.

We have a respiration rate of about 18 breaths per minute. Thus in the course of a day we breathe about 26,000 times — a number that corresponds to the much larger rhythm of the ice ages, which return every 26,000 years. It is also the number of the platonic year: the number of years it takes for the sun to return to the same position in the Zodiac. We know that the heart is intimately linked to breathing as part of our rhythmical system, because our heart beats about 72 times per minute, which can be calculated as four beats for each respiration. Here again we see that heart rate and breathing are related to a cosmic rhythm.

The pump theory is not based on a spiritual idea. If pressure is applied in a pump, water comes out. However, if the heart were to act as a pump there would be literally tons of substance which it would have to move around the body. The amount of blood pushed through our system is indeed enormous, and it would be quite impossible for such a small organ to deal with this amount of substance if there were not another force present.

Experiments have been done which show that the movement of the blood is also influenced by suction. The capillaries, which go into every cell, show a sucking force (etheric), not one which is pushing (astral). The cells demand to be nourished in the same way that the citizens in a city have to be nourished and therefore create a demand for the food which comes as nourishment — not the other way round.

Another point to be considered is that the heart is not an organ. Organs demand their own nourishment, but also contribute to it. They digest substance in order to gain sustenance. The heart, however, is a fourfold muscle: the chambers are linked to certain valves so that the content of what they contain is affected in a rhythmical way which provides sudden impulses. It is this stopping process which gives a jolt, as it were, to the heart — a momentary force that impels the movement of blood and that is responsible for blood pressure. Through this pressure the blood receives the force to push it forward, but the nearer it comes to the capillaries, the more it is influenced by suction. You have both blood pressure and pulse, but the main function is suction: the demand of the organs and the capillary cells at the periphery.

The heart is a regulator of, on the one hand, the astral forces which have to do with the closure of valves and, on the other hand, the etheric forces which have to do with the suction of the blood, drawing it into the blood vessels, which in their turn also provide enough energy for the blood to flow back to the heart. Of course, the world of the etheric is not yet clearly perceptible to scientists.

The heart also has a nervous system with two aspects: the vagus nerve on the one hand and the sympathetic nerve on the other. The sympathetic nerve excites or impels the heart, while the vagus has a calming, slowing effect. They both keep the rhythm in balance, though not regulating the pulse. In addition, the heart has a nervous system of its own — a kind of nerve knot, which regulates what goes on in the heart itself.

The embryo

If you examine the human embryo in the first 17 days after fertilisation, there is not yet any sign of a body. What is taking place is the formation of a house for the developing embryo, which is made up of the four sheaths that will later be discarded after birth. On the 18th or 19th day a flow of cells appears which will later become blood, and on the 24th day or thereabouts we see a small organ at some distance from this flow, which begins to develop and is the future heart. We therefore find that the future blood cells are already flowing before the heart is formed.

The heart is subject to the impulse of a rhythm — one which is regulated. This rhythm is not due to a mechanical force, but is a regular movement which adjusts itself — and this is interesting in relation to what happens if someone is given a new heart or a mechanical regulator. In such cases the result is an absolutely regular heartbeat, whereas in a normal heart the rhythm is adjusted to needs and conditions.

Culturally, many ideas are associated with the heart. It is seen as the seat of warmth and ideals, whereas the brain is 'a cold fish'. It is to the heart that we attribute our emotional life, and we may say that someone is 'good-hearted'. If the heart balances out the emotional life, then it follows that the heart is affected by emotional abnormalities. Blood pressure can go up. The heart can be affected by shock or bereavement or any such traumatic circumstances. We also link the heart to our feelings of love for one another. A warm heart leads to an equanimity of mood and a capacity for inner listening to see behind outer appearances, behind words, or whatever we see and hear in nature. It is through warmth that we try to reach beyond appearances, and thus we can regard the heart as a receptor of qualities which are in the realm of the etheric — of the spiritual, which exists behind outer appearances.

In this sense we can say that the heart is the true basis of communication in social intercourse. Healthy people rely on their heart in order to reach into the social environment with their warmth. The capacity to do this depends on the health of the heart.

What has this to do with adolescence and youth guidance?

During the time of puberty our constitution is changed physically, etherically and from the point of view of our astral/soul nature.

In childhood we internalise the etheric stream which comes with us and brings us into life, and at this stage we begin to take in the world from the point of view of astrality. How this happens is dependent on the experiences which we bring from our previous life on earth. During the embryonic stage we work strongly out of this previous karma, and our ego does not enter into the picture for a considerable time. A growing child, developing from birth to puberty, changes gradually and prepares himself for puberty, not only sexually, but from the point of view of overall maturity. Therefore, there are two births during childhood: the first is the natural birth; the second is the change of teeth, which is only an outer sign of the emergence of the etheric forces from the first seven-year period, which now become available for new processes in the child's development.

With these two steps, parts of our old etheric forces are changed and brought to bear on our new earthly nature. However, this does not apply to the heart. The new etheric forces, which we take in around the time of the change of teeth and which influence our other organs, do not affect the heart, and we have to wait until about 11 to 15 years of age for this next birth to happen, which we can describe as the change in the etheric heart.

Old forces are released into the universe and we receive new etheric forces to replace these astral elements which have been at work in the heart up to this point. This constitutes a third birth, which not only has to do with sex and maturity, but also with our impulses and whole destiny — our move from living out of the past into the future. We receive etheric forces, which have to do with what happened between our last death and new life and these are fruitful forces and represent a changeover which expresses itself in the 'flowering' of puberty.

Our former destiny begins to 'rumble on' out of our own past. Aspects of it appear and we have to incorporate happenings from our past into our present life. We need all our strength and courage to deal with this, and anorexia, violence etc. are manifestations of how young people cope with taking on the reality of their own destiny.

Because of this, we have no alternative but to turn to a young person with compassion, and with this we can say, 'Yes, you are violent, full of anxiety etc., but you are struggling to cope with your own destiny and have to find a way to transform yourself.' Young people are encountering forces they are barely conscious of, yet have to take on the implications of what in the end is very much part of them.

In order to help during this time, we have to occupy ourselves with questions of karma and reincarnation in our own life, as well as in the lives of others. We can help if we recognise that the supra-organic changes taking place at this time, and the appearance of inherited characteristics, which are strongly manifested in the change of the etheric and astral heart in the young person, need to be met with our empathetic understanding as this is a situation which belongs to the development of every human being, ourselves included.

The human heart is not a pump

From a thesis submitted to the Youth Guidance Course, January 1996

The organ of the heart

When I picked up a children's 'pop-up' book about the human body, two statements literally 'jumped' off the page: 'The brain is a computer' and 'The heart is a pump within the machine of the human body.' It saddened me to see the human body degraded in that way, especially in a book addressed to children.

Novalis spoke about the human body in quite a different way:

> There is only one temple in the world and that is the human body. Nothing is holier than this lofty form. A temple through which light and life can flow.[1]

When we look at the skeleton, discovering its beauty and mastery in the way each bone is formed and linked with another, it is easy to understand why Novalis would call the body a temple. The spirit seems almost to be visible.

I once taught a class of 14-year-olds about the human skeleton, and when the skeleton was shown, a boy with learning difficulties was especially impressed by the ribcage and sternum: 'It's like that thing in the hall!' he exclaimed. It took me a while to realise what he meant, but shortly afterwards, when I was in the chapel in Camphill Hall, it became apparent what he had been referring to (*see Figure 1 overleaf*).

Around that time, this same boy had attended a young people's service in which he heard that up until that point he had been guided and led by others — his parents and teachers —but that from now on he would begin to take responsibility for himself. A daunting prospect, especially for this young man, but the crucial step which we all make at this stage of life, to face the lifelong struggle and drama of our lives.

Figure 1
Camphill Hall, near Aberdeen, showing over-arching staircase
above the chapel, forming an enclosed space for the altar.

Half a year later I was teaching the same class about the blood circulation and the human heart. I was concerned that the ingrained idea of the heart as a pump might creep in, so we began every lesson with a dynamic drawing based on a simple diagram of blood circulation (*see Figure 2 opposite*). This was then transformed in the following way. The pupils traced the basic form of this diagram and entered into the rhythm of the pattern that was created. As they went over it again and again, a hush fell over the class. Eventually a shape with four parts and a gap in the middle appeared (*see Figure 3 opposite*).

After this exercise it was then possible to discuss the rhythmical flow of the blood — the systole and diastole of the heartbeat — and nobody mentioned the word 'pump'.

Walter Holtzapfel[2] describes how it is still widely accepted that the heart's function is that of a pump, although for physical reasons this is not tenable. Calculations have been made to determine the workload the heart would have to perform in order to pump blood through the fine capillaries: 20,000 kg per day during rest periods. This would be enough energy to lift 20 kg to the height of 1 km during the course of a day. Others have calculated an even greater workload: 500,000,000 kg per day. Obviously a heart muscle weighing 300 g could not produce so much energy.

Rudolf Steiner made a revolutionary statement,[3] namely that it is the blood that moves and forms the heart. In the early stages of embryonic development, the blood of the embryo is formed outside its body in the 'blood islands' of the yolk sac. From there it flows towards the embryo's body, through circulatory routes, forming a centre which begins to pulsate.

As the diagram in Figure 2 shows, four chambers of the heart are formed. The two smaller chambers above are the auricles, through which the blood flows before entering the larger chambers, the ventricles. The left auricle (*on the right in the diagram*) receives the oxygenated (red) blood from the lungs. This blood then flows through the left ventricle to the aorta, which distributes it to all parts of the body. When the de-oxygenated (blue) blood is carried through the veins back to the heart, it is led through the right auricle to the right ventricle and out through the pulmonary arteries to the lungs again.

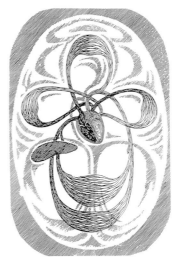

Figure 2
Human circulatory system.[4]

A complicated and ingenious system of valves, muscles and cusps ensures that the blood flows in the right direction, and that red and blue blood never mix (*see Figure 4 overleaf*). In fact the heart is not pumping but stopping the blood, giving it a new direction — a new impetus.

When my pupils were drawing the rhythmical form to which I referred above (*see Figure 3*), a certain rhythm in speed was noticeable. They

Figure 3

29

slowed down as they approached the centre, then gained a new thrust of energy after passing the centre. If you listen to a heart beating, a rhythm of short and long beats will be discernible — 'lub … dub, lub … dub' — the systole and diastole, or alternating contraction and dilation of the ventricles. Just this rhythm was noticeable while the pupils were drawing; they became calm and their breathing deeper. It is the space formed in the middle which

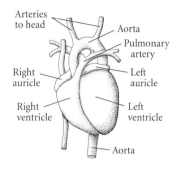

Figure 4
Mammalian heart

is important — a space which is clear, clean, empty, quiet. I believe that this space is to do with freedom.

Sun, warmth, soul and spirit

Our conception of what our heart is like is closely connected with how we think about the human being from the point of view of his spirit, soul and physical existence. Therefore it is of utmost importance that we teach this subject in the right way.

The heart is the organ of the human organism which is the most frequently referred to in daily conversation as well as in literature and poetry (somehow the liver and kidneys do not seem to have the same attraction to poets as the heart does). The heart is very often mentioned when feelings or spiritual qualities are being expressed.

It is clear how the soul affects the flow of blood: fear and anxiety cause the blood to withdraw from the periphery and the person becomes pale. The opposite often happens in response to anger, shame or happiness: the person blushes as the blood rushes to the surface of the skin. The blood belongs to the metabolic pole: its warmth, mobility and role in the exchange of substances in the tissues, as well as its faculty for constant regeneration, oppose it to the nerve–sense system.*

The heart is placed between these two polarities, bringing equilibrium and harmony, and always striving to restore balance. Heart illnesses are almost always secondary, and develop slowly as a result of extremes which become manifest in the nervous or metabolic systems.

The heart is placed at an angle of about 23 degrees relative to the spine, which is the same as the angle of the earth's axis relative to the sun. Solar rhythm is also inherent in the rhythm of the heartbeat: the average adult heart beats 72 times per minute, with four beats for every breath. This means that we breathe approximately 26,000 times in the course of the day, which is the number of years required for the sun's vernal point to complete the cycle through the Zodiac and return to the beginning again.

These numbers may seem static and far-fetched. However, the heart is often referred to as the sun within the human organism, and its relation to the element of warmth needs no further examples.

During the evolution and appearance of living creatures, as they developed from fish to reptiles and further to birds and mammals, the element of warmth entered gradually into the body from without. The temperature of the water determines the body warmth of fish; reptiles have a closed inner blood circulation which still receives its warmth from the surroundings. Birds and mammals have developed an individual self-regulated inner warmth. The human warmth organisation is almost independent of the surrounding conditions. Here we recognise a movement from outside to within that is similar to the development of blood circulation and the heart in the growing embryo. In the human being warmth becomes ever more inward, and the incarnation of the ego follows this inward direction.

In all the organs and the capillaries there is an exchange of substances with the blood, but not in the heart. In it the blood remains separate: there is no exchange of substance. In this way the heart does not come into direct contact with the outer world. This independence of the heart enables it eventually to become an organ for the ego.

---

* The nerve–sense system is concentrated in the head, as is our conscious life, even though it extends into our body. The metabolic system is focused in the digestive region and related organs, which carry out the whole process of metabolism. In contrast to the nerve–sense system it remains healthy as long as it functions in relative unconsciousness. Therefore a polarity is manifest in the human form between on the one hand the head — the sense–nerve system (thinking) — and on the other hand the digestion — the metabolic–limb system (will) — while in between lies the heart–lung/circulatory system (feeling/sensation).

The ego organ in the developing child

In a baby the heart beats very fast and irregularly. The young child's physical body is very closely linked with the etheric body, which he has brought along from the spiritual world. This can be observed in the young child's mirroring power. He absorbs everything that we do around him and reflects this back by imitating. He is unable to distinguish between good and evil, and learns this solely through the actions and reactions of adults around him.

Only when the child begins to experience himself as a separate person, and refers to himself as 'I', is he able slowly to begin to learn what is right and what is wrong. This function of the conscience in moral development is therefore at first totally dependent on the outer stimulation and is only slowly internalised.

At the age of 9–10 years the child often experiences a difficult time — a new feeling of loneliness, of isolation, can come about as he becomes more self-conscious and aware. At this time the heart grows in size, and its capacity for holding blood increases. At this age the heartbeat and breathing begin to settle into a rhythm in a ratio of four to one. This heightened awareness and self-consciousness is a strengthening of the ego consciousness, but the child is still far from certain and continues to need the support of trusting adults.

The way a child comes through this 'nine-year crisis' is very important for later life. Heart ailments in childhood often come to a peak at this time — such as rheumatic carditis, a severe illness which often leads to faults in the heart valves (such defects affect the heart's ability to keep the blood separate as it flows through the heart).

At puberty the heart passes through another crisis. Rudolf Steiner calls this time the time of 'earth maturity' — a sexual maturation but also a 'maturity of breathing'.[5] The ego consciousness of the adolescent develops into an earthly consciousness, awakens to matters and affairs of the whole earth.

In breathing we find the image of taking in the world around us, transforming it into our own organism and breathing out the transformed substance, giving something back to the world again. This image may explain the concept 'maturity of breathing', as the adolescent lives between the two extremes of being very outgoing, interested in the wider world and being inwardly self-absorbed and self-centred — another image of breathing.

During puberty the regularity and rhythm which was established around the age of nine is often upset. The pulse may suddenly accelerate and the blood pressure rise. Other heart ailments may develop during puberty. A particularly serious heart illness is Fallot's tetralogy, which prevents the separation of red and blue blood. If the heart is malfunctioning, proper (direct) contact with the earth cannot be established — which is particularly critical at this age, when 'earth maturity' should develop. Most youngsters with this illness do not survive this time, unless they are helped by surgical operations.

Near the beginning of this chapter I mentioned a dynamic drawing (*see Figure 3*) which demonstrated the importance of rhythm, and the space created in the centre. The fact that there is no exchange of substances in the heart, and that the polarities of blue and red blood flow opposite each other without mixing, gives the human being the possibility to face the self in self-consciousness. Walter Holtzapfel[6] explains that this is a freedom which only the ego is permitted. This independence of the ego enables the human being to raise himself above outer influences and be receptive to the voice of conscience. Therefore the wellbeing of the heart is the basis of our inner stability.

Etheric and astral in relation to the heart

In his lecture *The Human Heart*[7] Rudolf Steiner speaks in great detail and with vivid imagery about the incarnation of the 'etheric heart'. The following is an attempt to distil this lecture (which is well worth reading in full).

Rudolf Steiner describes the *etheric body* as a universe in itself. In its circumference there is something in the nature of stars, in its lower nature an image of earth. In the etheric body there is an image of the sun nature and the moon nature — a cosmic sphere complete with stars, zodiac, sun and moon.

Before birth — before the soul of the human being unites itself with the physical organism of the parents-to-be — the soul draws to itself the forces of the universal ether. One can thus imagine the growing embryo and very young child clothed in a star-like ether body. As the child grows these stars at the periphery fade a little, but they remain there up

Figure 5

until the time when the child's second teeth appear. After this time these stars are gradually transformed into rays. The stars dissolve away in the human ether body, becoming rays which come together inwardly within the human being. During the time between the change of teeth and puberty, the etheric body is intensely radiant, with rays streaming inwards from outside (*see Figure 5*).

At the time of puberty these rays will have grown together at the centre, forming a distinct etheric structure of its own. In the midst of this centre the physical heart is suspended. This gathered-up radiance becomes the true etheric heart, replacing the etheric heart previously received through inherited forces of the embryo. The first inherited etheric heart decays, and in its place comes the new, the true etheric heart, which is a faithful image of the cosmos. We can be reminded of blooming flowers: many flowers carry the imprint of a star, and by the time the flower has ripened into seeds, the surrounding embracing petals have mostly disappeared, leaving the seeds or bud enclosed at the centre.

The radiance described here is maybe what can be experienced in children between 7 and 13 years of age. In this phase they usually have an abundance of energy, and never tire of rhythmical activities, having a natural openness and joy that makes this a healthy and 'blessed' time.

Rudolf Steiner then proceeds to describe the *astral body*. The human being builds himself an etheric heart which is an image of the outer universe; in the astral body he brings with him an image of the experiences he has undergone between his previous death and present birth. Thus the astral body is highly individualised and differentiated.

By the time of puberty the astral body becomes less and less differentiated. All that is living in the astral body as a multitude of single forms and structures 'slips' into the physical organs — primarily those above the diaphragm, but eventually spreading to the abdominal organs through the arteries. By the time we have reached adulthood, our organs have impressed within them several forms of our astral body. Because the forms of the astral body are pressed into the organs, the astral body itself becomes more and more indefinite — it becomes more or less like a cloud of mist.

From the moment a child learns to speak and retain ideas, intelligent movements are increasingly retained in the astral body. New definitions slowly begin to come into the astral body, and after puberty this happens with greater intensity and regularity. All the human being accomplishes through actions of his arms and legs, or instructs others to do, and all activities which find expression in the outer world, are 'written' into the astral body. Thus our actions leave imprints and shape or reshape the astral body. Thereby, from puberty onwards, a central organ is being created in which all our doing, our human activity is centred. Our human activity becomes 'inserted' via the astral body into the etheric heart.

The etheric heart is formed out of the cosmos, the astral heart is formed by the human being's deeds, and these now become united. A cosmic aspect is joined to the karma of the human being.

Everything we do in our earthly life becomes connected to the cosmos, and when we die it will be once again led over into the universe. Our deeds therefore do not only concern ourselves. They form our astral body as well as our own future and that of the cosmos.

Within the astral entity lives the ego, which has a long evolution behind it. The astral body descends into the organs, and so does the ego: it spreads out into the organs and takes possession of them. At puberty the ego will unite inwardly and intensively with the blood circulation: via the lungs the ego gradually approaches the heart, finally to enter into the forms created by the etheric and the astral. (We noted earlier that certain steps in the development of the ego take place at the age of 9–10 years, and that a regular breathing rhythm is established, thus illustrating the connection between the ego and the lungs.) In this way moral and physical events are brought together in the human heart.

At death, we first separate from the physical body, and then from the etheric body, but the human being 'lives on' in his astral body and ego. These expand into the spiritual world, into the cosmos, releasing the deeds which have imprinted themselves in the heart during our earthly life. Our deeds can only imprint themselves once this earthly joining has taken place in the heart at puberty. Children therefore cannot as yet form future karma as their deeds are not yet imprinted in the heart.

Children, however, need protection so that they do not use up their etheric strength, and in order to build up their moral strength so that they are not overpowered by these powerful astral forces.

Many children grow up in exposed, over-stimulating and challenging situations — maybe in violent or split family situations. They may be abused, or be deprived of consistency and security from an early age. Adults around them may not be able to take responsibility for their own deeds let alone those of their children. All these influences tear the etheric body and leave the young child at the mercy of astral forces, not having the moral strength to cope with them.

There have recently been several cases where children as young as eight have committed dreadful crimes. We need to ask ourselves whether such children are acting out of experiences from their previous life. Are they to carry the responsibility of creating future karma at so young an age? Will their deeds imprint themselves in the astral heart too early? And will they need to meet these actions again after death?

The educators of such children have the task of consciously taking the responsibility upon themselves for these children's actions, in order to protect them from having to create their own future karma too soon. But is this possible? Can one person do this for another person? And if so, how?

Freedom and love

> Jesus was walking along a road with some of his disciples, when they saw a dead dog dying by the wayside covered with flies and rotting away. They turned away in disgust but Jesus said: 'Look, he has beautiful teeth.'[8]

Thoughts which are not ruled by the necessity of the outer world have achieved a degree of freedom. They are our very own thoughts which we have activated ourselves. In the process our will has become an active force within our thinking.

There are several kinds of love; two of these are *instinctive love* and *human love*. instinctive love is closely linked to our physical and emotional desires — we sense that something outside ourselves is controlling our drives. Human love not only makes us blind to the failings of the one we love, it also opens our eyes to their good qualities.

In the example above, Jesus does not react instinctively to a sense perception, but makes a conscious decision to look for what is beautiful in a situation where others are only seeing ugliness. Such moments of consciousness show how our actions and thoughts are related to one another. Thought-filled actions, as in the example above, enable us to develop a devotional approach to the world around, which can become love. Rudolf Steiner says:

> Freedom and love grow and develop together. Thinking that is permeated with will gives rise to actions that are truly free, actions filled with thought are wrought by love.[9]

This illustrates how love and freedom are deeply interlinked, and we know how important it is for young people to develop and strive for just these qualities. To do this is often a great struggle, and leads to an underlying turmoil in the inner (and outer) life of the adolescent. Youngsters long for, and demand, independence in their actions, but this may just be one way of seeking 'freedom in their thinking'. They long for a new closeness in relationships, which is often sought through sexual encounters — but a love for the whole of humanity is also developing, and youngsters need to find ways and means of expressing this all-embracing love through their thought-filled actions.

Guidance of youth

Once we have understood something of these concepts, we find ourselves facing the responsibility and challenge to act in such a way that our actions would be worthy of forming a beneficial future karma. We also have the responsibility of guiding youngsters who are just beginning to create their future into meaningful and true actions. In education this task can be addressed at different levels:

Through crafts

Crafts should involve the learning of new skills, enabling youngsters to transform a natural raw material into a beautiful and useful object. By the time they reach 14–15 years of age, youngsters thirst for this kind of activity. It gives them an opportunity to work towards forming something perfect by means of their own thought-filled actions.

Through art

In art, beauty comes about through the struggle between good and evil, light and dark. To be allowed and to dare to go into this struggle is very important. Says Dr Hildegard Gerbert:

> When admiring what is beautiful the human being unites with the creative powers that are alive in nature and in creative activity itself. Out of admiration for the beautiful, selfless love for truth and moral resolution can develop. The beauty reveals itself fully to everyone everywhere. However, the human being's sense organ for perceiving the beautiful develops as he makes the effort to understand beauty.[10]

This effort to understand nurtures the inner life of the young person, and helps to develop will activity in thinking. In the upper school it is therefore important for the youngster to be given the opportunity to appreciate art as well as practise technique and expression.

Through a widening and deepening interest in the world

Youngsters live with the existential questions of 'Who am I?', 'Where do I come from?' and 'What contribution can I make?' These questions can be addressed through all the subjects taught in the upper school in the Waldorf–Steiner Schools. In the humanistic subjects, science or environmental studies, an interest is kindled, and a love for the world at large and all human beings. At the same time exactitude is demanded in observations and description. Practical involvement is essential in order to help youngsters enter fully into the subject, take hold of it and learn from their own direct experiences.

During the turmoil of adolescence, when a youngster's own karma is linking with a cosmic dimension, he may very well feel like that little drop of water in the sweet river as it reaches the salty sea, fearing that he

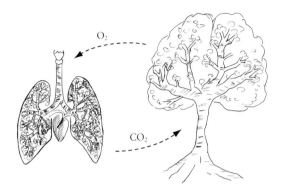

Figure 6

may disappear in the great bitter sea of adulthood, deprived of individuality and a feeling of self. It is therefore also important for each youngster to learn how he, together with every human being and the rest of nature, belongs and is an integral part of a whole world situation and time.

Coming back to the human heart and its link to the lungs, what better image can there be to convey just this message than the two 'trees' shown in Figure 6.

When the young lad mentioned at the beginning of this chapter recognised 'that thing in the hall' (*see Figure 1*) within the pattern formed in the human skeleton by the sternum (breastbone) and the ribcage which protects the heart, perhaps he recognised in a small way that he was part of a greater whole.

The service for young people which was held beneath that very 'thing in the hall' can be an image of the heart protected by the sternum. There life flows between the spiritual world of the far-reaching cosmos and our everyday earthly life. These two streams come extremely close together but they do not quite mix, just like the red and the blue blood. It is through the opposite qualities of these two streams that the ego of the human being can achieve freedom and express love.

Youth guidance and empathy

Youth Guidance Conference, Blairdrummond, Scotland, 8 November 1981

The individual in the period of adolescence is like a small boat leaving the security of a harbour and setting out to sea, full of the spirit of adventure. This boat has to pass through turbulence, as well as moments of calm and peace, before reaching dry land — in this case the more settled shore of adult life.

R. D. Laing, when writing about human behaviour in *The Politics of Experience*,[1] postulates that we see each other's behaviour but cannot perceive the experience of the other which underlies it. Thus 'experience is man's invisibility to man.'

If we appreciate what anthroposophy says about the human being, we cannot accept the finality of this statement, but we can use it as the point of departure for a path which sets out in an act of empathy to reach an experience of the other's experience.

Rudolf Steiner often spoke of the evolution of human attributes or faculties. He attributed the birth of the faculty of compassion to Gautama Buddha who, encountering the untold suffering in the world once he had finally left his sheltered home, was able to absorb this suffering into himself so that it became part of his inner experience.[2, 3]

The emergence of the internal voice of conscience sprang from the experience of Elijah on the mountain, when, having confronted the 450 prophets of Baal and called down the heavenly fire, he hears the Divine Voice, not from the realm of the elements without, but from the still, small voice within himself. Once such faculties emerge through the leaders of humanity, they gradually enter general human experience.

When considering sympathy and antipathy as Steiner described them, we see how they work in social life. In meetings between people there is a constant oscillation between sympathy and antipathy which is almost beyond our control. It is perhaps as little under our control as our breathing process. We 'sleep into the other' and reawaken to ourselves in rapid succession and alternation.

Gradually, however, as a furtherance of compassion and conscience, a new possibility has begun to emerge in human experience, which is that of empathy: a new power, a potential for holding still this eternal oscillation between sympathy and antipathy in the same way that we can also hold our breath; and in this deed of holding still, a space — a gateway — is opened towards the other person and his experience. This ability relies on a strenuous and meditative activity which leads towards the private world of the other one — into his *Sein* (state of being) — and creates an experience of his experience.

However, to attain this faculty we have to strip off all illusions about ourselves — all functional relationships (teacher–pupil, doctor–patient, etc.). We must even strip ourselves of our own wish to help. In this way empathy is almost a non-power — the non-power of the consciousness-soul. It is the outcome of a meditative path — the way leading into the landscape of the other person, into his sanctuary. Communities with therapeutic aims need to cultivate and include this path in their work if they are to exercise an effective curative influence on those who seek help from them.

This striving for empathy gives to the adolescent the experience that the ocean over which he is sailing is also surrounded by dry land. But, to offer this quality of being dry land beyond the often stormy seas, simply to *be* it, we must be able to work on our attitudes, to lay aside our 'educator' function and, at least for a while, to learn to walk on the water in a figurative but also a real way, and to be with the adolescent in his boat, keeping him company, being at his side when the storm rages.

With this description of empathy we can feel how it is connected to Steiner's description of mankind's development. Today we are already exposed to a light which streams in from the future, from a sixth epoch.* In future it will be impossible not to experience the experience of the other.

---

* Rudolf Steiner attributed seven epochs, or phases, to the present stage in the development of human consciousness. Christianity began in the fourth epoch, and the fifth epoch started with the Renaissance. Characteristics of the fifth epoch are individualisation and the growth of scientific materialism. The sixth epoch will see the possibility of a greater materialism as well as the opening for an expansion of consciousness, which is already spoken of today as something to be attained.

We have a moral commitment not to be as Laing says we are — although initially we are. It is our prejudices which shape our experience of the behaviour of the other, and it is just these that we have to overcome, to surpass.

The judicial system of today is rooted in the experience we have of each other, which goes back 2,000 years. It is rooted in revenge. But today, because of the Deed of Christ, and the working of the Christ Impulse in history, this approach should be totally meaningless. Instead of revenge we are evolving step by step towards expanding not only perception but also the power of forgiveness — and with that a marked change will occur over the next 2,000 years and we are already involved in this process. This has to do with the development of the spirit self.* Gradually we become responsible for the other person's experience, but our first lesson is not to learn how to help, but to learn how not to cause, and this is because of the initial invisibility of the other's experience which leads us to so easily hurt and damage those whom we love.

The College Meeting

In our encounters with adolescents, consideration of empathy can lead us to look afresh at the potential of the College Meeting.† 'Therapeutic talks' are often found to be beneficial. They may take place on a one-to-one basis, or at other times the young person might choose two or three people — students, trainees or adults — to join in a talk to give it a dimension in which they can both speak and listen.

Some therapeutic establishments have established such talks on a weekly basis, for instance, and often an adolescent's peers are better able to help than even an experienced adult co-worker. Some places have had College Meetings on developmental issues, such as Down's syndrome or autism, drawing on experiences and observations taken from life.

We become aware of the distinction we need to make between

---

* The spirit self refers to a stage in inner development, reached when the ego of the human being has worked on the realm of desire and self-interest to such an extent that the self can be said to have been spiritualised, purified.

† A College Meeting can be held on many issues, including the needs of an individual such as a child or young person. The situation will usually be one giving rise to concern and where fresh insight is required. The meeting will look at the history and present circumstances of that situation in a concentrated and structured manner, with the aim of identifying any necessary therapeutic measures.

coping with difficulties as they occur and enhancing our understanding. It is obviously necessary to do both, and it can be a help to look again at the three pillars of Camphill described by Dr Karl König in his book *The Camphill Movement*,[4] these being the College Meeting, the Bible Evening and the attempt to practise the Fundamental Social Law in community living. In this context the College Meeting can be the source for our spiritual life — the wellspring for the fire of wisdom which flows into and enlivens seminars, study groups etc.

Viewed in this light, College Meetings do not take place in order to change the destiny of the child or young person, but in order to help us — in order to stimulate our own change. And if we manage to develop our experiences of the young person, then our attitude towards that person will change. He can be freed from our misconceptions and granted the space to change out of his own necessity and potential. This is the magical element of the College Meeting — that we change our attitude and encourage the other one to become himself despite what might be his manifest difficulties. Of course, we must remember that the real effect of such a College Meeting manifests itself in the night when the individual approaches and reviews in sleep his innermost relationship to his own destiny.

In this way the College Meeting fosters our willingness to change in such a way that we can avoid becoming the cause of strain and breakdowns for other people. The first thing we have to learn is not to cause, and the College Meeting is there to teach us this. What then follows is the opportunity to develop an enhanced level of understanding of the other as well as ourselves, freeing the child and the young person or adult to become truly who they are and want to be.

Empathy I

7 November 1971

Empathy is a word which has been used fairly frequently over the last few decades. We can probably include this word when thinking of the tremendous change that R. D. Laing's work has brought about in the understanding of psychiatric or mental illness. In any textbook on psychiatry up until the late 1950s, mental illness, schizophrenia or psychosis were conditions in which a person dropped out of a context that was humanly understandable — he became 'insane'. We can imagine that at any moment there were hundreds of thousands of people on earth who were regarded as being completely and incomprehensibly 'mad'. This was the universally held view, but it is different now. The possibility of looking at situations differently is due to the emergence of the faculty of empathy, which enables not only psychiatrists but also so-called lay people to be more understanding towards their fellows, and certainly towards those who manifest problems and disorders.

Having drawn on what I have absorbed of Rudolf Steiner's teaching in my approach to the theme of empathy, the first question I would ask is whether or not empathy is the beginning of what he describes as the natural psychological condition which man will attain in the sixth epoch* — the condition of total compassion. He said that with changes of human consciousness over time, the human mode of experience within the next few thousand years will increasingly turn towards a condition where we will be unable to witness the suffering of another person without experiencing it as if it were our own.

Whatever we might say about present-day problems compared to those of the early part of this century, there is a remarkable increase in the effective influence of compassion. In those days almost everyone

* See footnote on the seven epochs in the previous chapter (page 42).

seemed to accept as inevitable the idea that some people would always be poor. They were there, and this was felt by any normal person to be the accepted state of affairs. It was part of the world, and because of it millions were destined to die of starvation in countries such as China and India. This way of thinking is now unacceptable to the vast majority of people, not for any specific ideological reasons, but because they feel differently about it. In the mid-19th century, slavery was still a matter of course, and earlier the sublime ideals of Plato's Republic arose out of a society based on slavery. I mention these things to indicate that there are natural progressions in human evolution — in this case towards compassion and social conscience. We can probably assume that the phenomenon of empathy has to do with this general development.

Empathy in its full meaning is not simply a feeling, or just a question of putting oneself into the other person's situation. It has a therapeutic connotation as well as a cognitive one. It is an understanding that arises out of an effort of feeling. In the therapeutic context I am reminded of Rudolf Steiner's description of empathy in the second lecture of his course on curative education,[1] in which he speaks about the various conditions met in children with developmental difficulties, and creates a foundation for curative education as a practice based on therapeutic understanding. He says the following:

> If the teacher can feel his way right into the situation of the child, if he is able in himself to feel what the child feels, and at the same time out of his own effort to evoke in his soul a deep compassion with the child's experience, then he will develop in his own astral body an understanding for the situation the child is in, and will gradually succeed in eliminating in himself all subjective reaction of feeling when faced with this phenomenon in the child. By ridding himself of every trace of subjective reaction, the teacher educates his own astral body.

I could not put this any better or more clearly. It is a concise description of empathy and indicates what is required for a therapeutic educational approach.

Rudolf Steiner stresses that in order to be helpful to the child we must 'wipe out sympathy as well as antipathy' in order to gain differentiation in our understanding and experience. In the psychology of today we speak of the ambivalence of emotions that, despite our avowed love for someone else, also hurt them. If we think that as long as a person loves, all will be well and no harm will be done, then a situation arises where our development is halted.

Having talked about wiping away these traces of sympathy and antipathy, of subjective reaction to the child's situation, by working on ourselves, Rudolf Steiner comments that as long as the teacher or person engaged with the child has a sympathetic or antipathetic reaction to the child's situation, then 'so long will he remain incapable of making any real progress with him.' He then goes on to say:

> Not until the point has been reached where a phenomenon to do with the child becomes an objective picture and can be taken with a certain calm and composure as an objective picture for which nothing but compassion is felt; not until then is the necessary mood of soul present in the astral body of the teacher. Once this has come about, the teacher is there by the side of the child in a true relation and will do all else that is needful more or less rightly.[2]

A further help in understanding what 'wiping out sympathy and antipathy' means is found in Rudolf Steiner's lecture cycle *A Psychology of Body, Soul and Spirit*.[3] Here he speaks of sympathy and antipathy as the two primary forces active in our soul life. He makes a tremendous effort to help us get away from the idea that they have to do with the feelings known as sympathy and antipathy. He describes the force of sympathy as having to do with the will, whereas the force of antipathy is related to our intellectual life. The force of antipathy is related to our central nervous system and therefore to death processes. From the moment of our first breath, not one new nerve cell is born — indeed, every day hundreds of thousands of nerve cells die. That is only the case with nerve cells; all the other cells in the body multiply and can be replaced. We therefore grow and put on weight because cells other than those in the nervous system can multiply so that our organ systems develop. There is only the one organ system — that to do with the nerves — which functions on a different basis and is related to death instead of renewal.

With concepts like these, Rudolf Steiner has given to the world the possibility of extending our understanding of the human being in a radical way, and if such ideas were used it would advance our self-knowledge, as well as our psychology, in a tremendous way.

In psychoanalysis, Freud tried to describe this polarity of the soul, but we need to supplement his ideas with what can be gained from anthroposophy. For instance, in describing this polarity, Freud did not use the terms sympathy and antipathy, but the 'id', which was the entirety of instinctual life and included the libido (or sympathy and love), and an opposing force which he called 'thanatos', the death drive. Steiner indicated that our consciousness is not a phenomenon of our life function, but of the 'death' force present within our life. I know of no other writer, philosopher or psychiatrist having said that consciousness is based on the death processes in us and quite physically on the nervous system, which is why when all brain cells die a person immediately loses consciousness. On the other hand, we observe that when we breathe pure oxygen, the death process is halted — but no one thinks of these things in terms of consciousness, because we are beset with the idea that consciousness is produced by the body, meaning it is the brain which excretes thoughts in the same way that kidneys excrete urine.

In his third lecture on curative education,[4] Rudolf Steiner speaks about morality, and does so in a unique way. He says we do not bring morality with us into our life. Thoughts, he says, can never be wrong because they are universal and cosmic in origin. What can happen, though, is that we mirror (and hence express) them in a distorted way. Nevertheless, by themselves they are always right. He goes on to say that when we are born we have in us our will, which has no inherent rightness or morality, for morality has to be acquired and built up on earth. What we have acquired as morality in our former incarnations is used up between death and rebirth when we are concerned with building up our body:

> Ethics and morality have to be acquired anew in each single earthly life. This has a very significant result, namely, that inasmuch as we come from pre-earthly existence without morality, we have to develop intelligence in our will. We enter with our will into our organs, and in our will we must develop intelligence for what is brought to us in the way of ethics and morality. We must develop a 'sense' for it … It is quite wonderful, how moral and ethical impulses pour into the child when he is learning to speak.

At first it might seem that Steiner means specific moral codes. But the concepts of karma and reincarnation would suggest that if, for example, my previous incarnation was 2,000 years ago, what was moral then would probably not be so today, and in this way I cannot bring appropriate moral codes with me into this life. However, Rudolf Steiner is not referring to the contents of morality, which are relative to the age in which we live, but rather the sensitivity for understanding the moral codes which result from what we experience as the morality and codes of conduct which we find around us. Steiner says that this sensitivity comes about as the small child is learning to speak.

In his lecture cycle *The Foundations of Human Experience*[5] Steiner describes how the forces of sympathy and antipathy must meet, and how the acquisition of speech and language is the most specific integration of these two forces. He says that these forces are by themselves neither good nor bad, but are simply forces. He describes how the force of sympathy is both love and hate, aggression and destruction. It is simply will. The force of antipathy is not will, but mirroring, and this makes the contrast clear and shows that the former is bound up with life and the latter with death. The one is being, the other not being. This distinction can help us to understand empathy in a better way. By feeling ourselves into a mirror, we experience it as being something still, smooth, cold and totally exposed. It does not accept anything. Everything which crosses its path is reflected back. This is an image of the force of antipathy — a force that does not go against or towards, but is something on its own, is closed off — and this closed-off-ness is needed if we are to achieve a degree of clear, exact mirroring of the world and each other. The force of sympathy, on the other hand, is outgoing. Love, sympathy, aggression and devouring make manifest the taking hold, the having of aims, the continuous doing and undoing which is present in life. As the two basic forces of our soul existence, sympathy and antipathy, must become integrated, they each require transformation and integration. And with this (in some ways this happens quite naturally) our thinking, our emotions and our actions already represent an integration of these two forces.

The original idea of morality in Freudian theory had to do with the three-cornered relationship between mother, father and child. This is described in the age-old myth of Oedipus, and it is helpful to realise that

Freud, in his treatment of neurotic patients, found that the vast majority of cases seemed to show inner conflicts and problems arising out of the fact that those involved did not trust their own capacity for love. They were uncertain about it, and some developed mechanisms for self-punishment, such as those found in certain types of neurosis. At the root of it, patients described situations, usually with their parents in quite early infancy, which they couldn't really master. From his cases, Freud concluded that the Oedipus saga is not only a majestic story, but is the description of an unavoidable, perhaps even necessary situation — namely that the young, helpless child experiences that there are certain possessive qualities within his natural love for his mother, and that these bring him into conflict with his father, although he also loves him. He is put into a difficult situation in which conflict gives rise to the beginnings of guilt.

Normally this conflict resolves itself, and we derive our potential for morality from learning to cope with the fact that our love contains elements that are necessarily negative. An infant's love for his mother is primary. It is not love in the sense in which St Paul used the word (see below) but a biological instinctive love, which has its roots in the force of sympathy — a sympathy which is there long before it is mitigated by the force of antipathy, by reflective thinking. If this process goes wrong, it can lead to both illness and complex problems. But if all goes well, we acquire the ability to feel guilt, to feel that some things are good and others bad. We are not born with this ability, but rather we develop it through our mastery of the Oedipal situation, in our transcending and understanding that our love contains aggressive, negative elements, and that as creative beings we also have to endure conflict. If we learn to deal with this primary human situation, then we can mature, and mature morally.

In his course of lectures on curative education[6] Rudolf Steiner described how the source for the power of empathy is inherent in the maturation process — present in our learning to tolerate and accept the ambivalence of primary forces that are present and active within us. Love is a primary force, but if it is not sublimated, differentiated and tempered by our understanding, it can also be aggressive and destructive. If this were not the case it would not be a force.

There is a statue by Henry Moore which can appear disturbing (*see*

Figure 7
Henry Moore. *Mother & Child**

Figure 7). It is of a mother with her infant. The infant is formed like a pecking bird with a wide-open beak and is held at a distance by the mother. Moore created many Madonna and Child images, but this particular one points to what I have described as the untempered and necessary elements of love. These can be subconscious, but a real mastery and conscious handling of the force of empathy can only arise out of our consciousness of the ambivalence of our basic emotions.

We must come to understand that our love can also hurt another person. There is no assurance that because we have goodwill we can only bring about pleasure. This is a childish idea. To the extent to which we have learned to understand that our love can cause pain to others, thus far can we extend empathy to others and also help them to cope as well. In learning to understand and tolerate the ambivalence of our emotions — an ambivalence that is unavoidable and necessary — we can also accept it in others, without blaming them and without meaning to show them where they have gone wrong.

* Bronze sculpture, 1953. Reproduced by permission of the Henry Moore Foundation.

Empathy is not a primary force — it is the achievement of maturity, of a tempering of the forces of sympathy and antipathy. St Paul already knew this and described it in a most brilliant and wonderful way. I shall therefore conclude this chapter by attempting to re-express his words from the point of view of empathy:[7]

While love is often impatient,
  empathy is patient.
While love is often aggressive,
  empathy is kind.
While love is often jealous,
  empathy envies no one.
Love is often proud,
  but empathy is never boastful, nor conceited.
While love is often selfish and easily takes offence,
  empathy is never selfish and never takes offence.
Empathy keeps no score of wrongs, does not gloat over men's sins,
  but delights in the truth.
There is nothing empathy cannot face.
There is no end to its faith, its hope and its endurance.

Empathy II

Youth Guidance Course, Pennine Camphill Community, 5 March 1995

Empathy is a soul force which we need to become aware of and try to understand if we are involved with adolescents. We can't expect *them* to have it, but for those of us who are around adolescents it is very important to develop it ourselves.

Ideally, at around the age of 21, the ego is born in the individual, and the task becomes one of taking possession anew of the body which forms its home. The task of the ego is to become the master of the soul forces and to direct what is to happen afterwards in later life.

The initial phase of education comes to an end at 21. Up until this time the stimulus for education has come from outside, through teachers, friends etc. At 21 individuals have to enter the phase of self-education. Teenagers think that life should go on in the same way, but by the time they reach 21 something changes: a new beginning is made, and from then onwards, development will only take place through their own efforts.

In adult life, new and different aspects of the soul forces are experienced through the activity of the ego. As the ego works on the astral body the sentient soul is formed; as it works on the ether body the mind soul is formed; and as it works on the physical body the consciousness soul is formed.

Ages 21–28: from the astral body arises the sentient soul.
Ages 28–35: from the ether body arises the mind soul.
Ages 35–42: from the physical body arises the consciousness soul.

This is the reverse process from what was begun at birth. It is the task of the ego, based on what has been achieved during the years up to 21, and as a result of our education, to keep on saying 'I have to acquire!' In a certain way, we have to be egoistic and self-centred, even up to the age of 42, if we are to find out what we are meant to do or study, or if we are to succeed in our work, and go through the experiences of falling in love, perhaps marrying, having a family etc. All these things benefit us rather than other people up to the age of 42, so that in the widest sense the time between birth and 42 could be called the egoistic period of life.

However, by the age of 42, when the soul forces explained above have been developed, a new awareness begins to show itself through which we can turn instead towards the world. We are gradually able to be less concerned about ourselves, and an attitude of interest appears, by means of which we can start to serve the world. We can start to pass on tasks, to help those who are younger to establish themselves. Feelings of love can be transformed into new qualities. Sexuality and family relationships are affected by a new force. Distance is gained from our own and our family's needs.

Through the development of the sentient soul and the mind soul, a new ability to think will emerge and affect our feeling life. This helps us to become more selfless and to develop a social quality of love. That is why at the age of about 42 a more truly social time of life begins, as our ego can gradually move its emphasis away from its focus on the soul, reaching out towards others in genuine interest and sociability.

What do we mean by the word 'love'?

The word 'love' has a positive note to it. I love my family, friends, nation etc. and this can indeed be very positive. But love can also have a negative side, offending and damaging others even if it is filled with good intentions.

I am aware of a need to express love, but I am not aware of how the other person is affected by what I do out of love. Love can become possessive, selfish. My need to love means that I do not necessarily question whether the other person wants to receive love, and then if the other person does not respond to my love, it can even turn into hate and anger.

Because of this, parents can be quite unhelpful towards their children and difficult situations may develop. It can be shocking to realise this — to realise that my love can damage the other person whom I say I love, as I feel that what I do is done out of these good intentions.

Sympathy and antipathy

Rudolf Steiner talked about sympathy and antipathy in at least two of his lecture courses.[1,2] Sympathy is usually regarded as positive and antipathy as negative. However, Rudolf Steiner described antipathy in relationship to the nervous system, the head and thinking forces which come out of the past. Antipathy enables us to adopt a certain distance from the world — to create a mirror which reflects without being involved. It is a non-involved activity of the head, and not in a negative sense. It is very important and enables us to keep our distance — to observe.

Sympathy is the polar opposite. It is related to the blood, to the will, to a force leading into the future through our deeds. Our will keeps us involved in the world. We cannot say it is only to do with our positive feelings, as it also has to do with negative feelings, which are also involved in what we do. We are involved through our love, care, our embracing, but also through our anger, having a temper, an outburst. Here the involvement is very strong. That is the main feature of sympathy — involvement with the world.

Neither pole is better than the other. Antipathy means standing back, reflecting; sympathy being involved. Some people are always involved; others are always standing back. We need to find a balance, a harmony and a rhythm between the two. It is like the breathing: breathing in and breathing out.

Love can be destructive, and our task is to become aware of this and then to work on its transformation. This is a task for the ego — the work it is meant to do. Thomas Weihs calls the two forces of sympathy and antipathy primeval. It is the force of empathy which makes a totality out of our soul forces, and creates a healthy balance between what can otherwise become polarising elements.

Empathy

What is needed is to develop the ability to become still inside, to still our soul forces, to begin to experience this balance. It is a balance which no longer experiences sympathy or antipathy or our own feelings. Your own feelings do not react to what is perceived. It is like holding one's breath between breathing in and breathing out. It is not something you can do constantly. You hold back your reaction, cease judging and instead become totally open to the experience of the other person. You become so still that you sleep into the other person and can begin to sense their experience. What is important is not to react in a polarised way to what we perceive, but to become still, alert, holding the balance.

There are two factors: compassion and understanding. Compassion relates to our feeling life, to the astral body; understanding to our thinking. Both have to be transformed by the quality of empathy. To perceive the other person and what that person needs and experiences, so that you are able to find a way to help, requires you to become guided by the needs of the other person and not by your own need to find an answer yourself, or to force your own viewpoint onto that other person. It is a process of perceiving without judging or wanting the other one to change. We cannot expect the adolescent to develop this yet. It is only possible later on, as we approach the age of 42, and is closely connected to the development of the consciousness soul.

Ages 35 to 42

During this mid-life period the physical body starts to decline. As we approach 42 we face a decision: whether to go the way of the body into frailty and decline, or whether to build an inner life which is strong enough to lift us above this decline. It is an autumn experience. If we fail to cope with it, we may fall into hopelessness and depression. Through the strength of our inner life we can turn to the world and use what we have developed, and primarily our experiences, to become concerned with more important things than ourselves and our own perspectives.

Mid-life calls for a step in individual development. At this time there is insecurity, doubt and questioning: 'Can I really do anything meaningful in the world?' There is loneliness and a tendency to revert to youthful pursuits. Our former convictions desert us and there is a need to find new values. All these factors bring about inner turmoil and sometimes outer turmoil as well.

Similar questions exist for the adolescent. Mid-life is often called the second adolescence, but by that time we should be better equipped to deal with the problems — better than we were at 16 or 20 years of age.

Youthful forces have to be replaced by conscious attitudes. The challenge of the consciousness soul is to bring the forces of thinking, feeling and willing together so as to find a new direction. We are in the fifth post-Atlantean epoch,* in which the consciousness soul is to be established as a faculty in mankind. Humanity is at a threshold. Do we go forward with our materialistic conception of life, or can we find a new spiritual dimension? It is the question facing the world: 'Is there a way into the future?' We ask this at the same time as we see so much crisis, fear and chaos. But we cannot answer such questions of today by only reacting out of sympathy or antipathy. What is needed is to establish the force of empathy as a third element. Some individuals who represent our present time have already expressed this new faculty:

1   Swiss writer Max Frisch did so in his play *Andorra*[3] and in his book *I am not Stiller.*[4] In both of these works a group of people make a judgement concerning another person. They are unwilling to give him a chance. They make over-hasty judgements and the result is destructive.

2   Brian Keenan, in *An Evil Cradling,*[5] his account of his experiences as a hostage in Beirut, describes how he experienced the feelings of his tormentor when he was beaten and abused by him, and could put them into context, even understanding them. He could free himself from his own fear and hate, and arrive at compassion towards his oppressor, experiencing him as the victim and the real prisoner.

The crisis of our time can only be overcome if this new attitude of empathy can appear as a transformation of what up to now we have described as the force of love. Blood ties — links of family, race and nation — have to be transcended so that we can recognise the individual and essentially human quality of the other person. It is a fundamental attitude of Christianity to take active steps to give the other person his freedom, not to impose my will or power over him.

We can find the best description of empathy recorded in so-called 'near-death' experiences, when people meet a being of light who embraces them in total love and total recognition of all their mistakes, yet without judgement. Raymond Moody in his book *Life after Life*[6] refers

---

* See footnote on the seven epochs in a previous chapter (page 42).

to the experiences of many people who had near-death experiences and reported an overwhelming feeling which could be summed up as 'I was totally known and totally loved.'

To have had this experience, despite knowing that faults and failures were also visible, was to have experienced the overwhelming presence of the reality of empathy. We can only strive towards this possibility, to bring it out of the realm of such spiritual experiences as are described above, into the realm of the human and social — to face the many situations we come across in daily life, and to respond, not with like or dislike, but with perceptive and effective empathy.

Insights into mental disorders
in adolescence

Youth Guidance Conference, Blairdrummond, Scotland, 8 November 1981

In order to understand the pathologies which can appear in adolescence, there are two critical phases in child development that we need to consider. We can start to shed some light on these two phases by looking at the myth of the creation as presented in Genesis, the first book of the Bible.

According to Genesis, humanity underwent not one but two creations. In the first chapter, we read how God created heaven and earth, then light and darkness, the sea and the dry land, and so on. Then in verses 26 and 27, we hear that God created man in His own image; mankind is created in the image of God. As yet there is no differentiation of the sexes; we are presented with the archetypal androgynous human being.

At the beginning of the second chapter of Genesis, there is no mention of man, and in the fifth verse we read that 'there was no man to till the ground.' We then discover that God created man a second time out of the dust of the earth, and that into man's nostrils He breathed the breath of life.

The first story describes man's archetypal creation, the second his physical, bodily creation. These two elements — the archetypal and the bodily — continue to affect human beings at many different levels. We find them, for instance, in embryonic development and again in child development. Let us first look at how they affect the latter.

The first chapter of creation

First there is the dawn of the birth of the ego, which, as Rudolf Steiner often pointed out, a child experiences in his third year of life — or rather it *used* to happen in the third year. At the present time, however, children's development has somehow accelerated, so that the ego birth begins between the 18th month and the third year of life. This means that in children today, the period leading up to this first ego experience has been foreshortened by over 30 percent. This is probably one of the most dramatic changes in the human state in our time.

By contrast, the onset of puberty has been brought forward by only about 10 percent. Puberty sets in between the ages of 12 and 14, which is not so dramatic a change as that affecting the early ego experience.

Rudolf Steiner said that this ego experience in childhood, which is a first step towards the interiorisation of the ego, is a Luciferic achievement.* It probably lies at the root of childhood autism, and is connected with the archetypal creation of man as it is related in the first chapter of Genesis.

A child of two or three lives in a world of meaning and of fantasy — in a world of myth. His experience is not yet confined to his body. It has not yet been narrowed down and predetermined by his bodily existence. He experiences his primary existence in the world of myth.

Around the second year, however — sometimes a little earlier, sometimes a little later, but while he is still living in a world of meaning — a child goes through some tremendously powerful experiences of shame, which are often more intense than anything he will experience later on. These feelings of shame are brought on in particular by the beginning of toilet training. Up until this point, his faeces were a most welcome thing to his mother. A full nappy, after all, showed that everything was working well. But suddenly it has become something that is disgusting and unwanted. This is incomprehensible to a small child, and the shame he experiences is surprisingly intense.

All this happens at the same time as a child experiences the approach of his own potential divinity in the realm of meaning — when for the first time he perceives that 'I am I'. It is an overwhelming experience — the more so as it is simultaneous with the experience of shame. If a child is already a frail child — vulnerable, weak and possibly neglected — or if his environment is not supportive enough, then panic can set in. In

---

* Lucifer is one of two higher beings (the other is Ahriman) who once detached themselves from those spirits who stood for the progressive development of earth and humanity, and who try, each in his own way, to oppose man's true moral and personal development. Lucifer tries to discourage man from adapting adequately to the earth's physical laws, thereby preventing him from fulfilling his true tasks.

this state of fear, a child can say 'no' to his own egohood — to his own approaching potential divinity. Childhood autism is characterised by this rejection of the child's own 'I'. It is the avoidance of ego endowment, and ultimately of becoming.

This is not a schizophrenic condition; it is the childhood condition that corresponds to schizophrenia later on. It is interesting to note that childhood autism was once called 'the schizophrenic syndrome in childhood'. All this constitutes the first chapter of the process of ego incarnation.

The second chapter of creation

The second chapter takes place in adolescence. The young person has now left the land of myth — of fantasy and meaning — and is now confronted with his body. This is the second crisis point in a person's ego experience, and is entirely related to his bodily existence. In this situation the differentiation between male and female plays a predominant role.

The challenge to the young person now is to say 'yes' to his ego — to his potential divinity — but this time within the realm of his physical body. His first encounter with his ego occurred when he was still in the realm of myth and could experience his ego without regard to his body. But this time his body is an all-important factor. There is a tremendous problem implicit in this second ego experience. For the young person has to say 'yes' to having been created in the image of God, while at the same time he is in a body that is very remote from any divine state.

At the beginning of adolescence — usually around the 12th year — a child begins to see his parents and other adults differently from before. He no longer sees them in mythological terms. They descend from the realm of myth, and all their human frailties, peculiarities and weaknesses become obvious. This is a tremendous experience for a young person. If all goes well, he will find compassion and forgiveness within him. His parents are no longer superior mythological beings but mere human beings. This is a difficult time for the parents as well. Their continuing parenthood depends on how much compassion and support their son or daughter can extend to them. (Perhaps it is just as difficult for a teacher in curative education to understand mental illness as it is for a parent to accept the forgiveness of his child.)

I clearly recall my own experience of my father when I saw him for the first time, not as a father but as a human being. It was at the supper table, and outwardly nothing much happened. He was sitting at the end of the table eating his soup and bread, and there was a drop of soup on his chin. This had probably happened many times before, but I experienced its significance for the first time, and realised that he needed my understanding and compassion.

Adolescent tensions and pathologies

At the age of 15 or 16, the young person reaches a peak in his intellectual ability and brain activity which is never surpassed. The brain as a cognitive organ attains the peak in its level of functioning. But at this stage there is a tremendous gap between an adolescent's intelligence and his experience of life. Very often he will be more intelligent than his father, who on the other hand is the more mature in experience — and this can result in problems.

Altogether, a tension exists between a young person's potentially divine ego and his bodily limitations — between his existence as a creator and his existence as a creature. We may suffer it, but are not yet accepting of the near-incompatibility of these two poles of our existence. Yet each one of us has to realise that he is a creator, but that at the same time a creature with all the limitations that go with creature existence.

During this period in adolescence, the youngster's environment is of the greatest importance. He needs to be affirmed, appreciated and supported, otherwise he may end up in an impossible situation and pathologies may develop. At this stage, however, he is still much more creator than creature, and if it appears impossible to reconcile the two, either the body element will be sacrificed or he will hit out destructively at his environment.

In the light of this insight, maladjustment can be seen as a negative reaction to the environment. Such maladjustment may often be quite mild, but it may also border on the psychopathic. Indeed, the impossibility of living a creature existence within a hostile, threatening environment may trigger a whole range of reactions, from the mildest maladjustment to the more severe psychopathic conditions.

Young people may manifest a total despair, the nature of which they are not even conscious of, by destructively hitting out at everything around them. It is astonishing to witness how far a person can be driven by such total despair. I am reminded of an incident from my days as a farmer. One year we had a problem with rats. They were everywhere and got me ever so annoyed by making themselves at home in our hay. One day I went into the byre and there, of course, was a rat. I was determined to show this creature who was master and chased it into a corner. I can still remember how the cornered rat looked at me and suddenly, with a big leap, went for me. This tiny creature, driven into an impossible situation, leapt at me against all odds. Young people can react in a similar way if they feel hemmed in by irreconcilable tensions.

Other adolescent pathologies

Apart from these reactions to the environment, a whole range of other conditions can be recognised as belonging to the pathologies of adolescence. They may include obsessions and neurotic states such as washing obsessions, overeating, refusal to eat, anorexia and so on. However, they may also include psychotic, manic and schizophrenic conditions as well. All of these correspond to childhood autism insofar as they appertain to the process of ego interiorisation. While some conditions ranging from maladjustment to psychopathy can be helped through our power of empathy, these other conditions — obsessive, neurotic, psychotic or schizophrenic — cannot be reached through our empathetic understanding (although the unconventional psychiatrist R. D. Laing has shown a way to understand the psychotic condition).[1]

Perhaps these latter conditions reveal an attempt to sacrifice the body or parts of it. The young person unconsciously seeks a partial death of the body as a consequence of failing to reconcile the creator with the creature existence. In schizophrenia this is characterised by a fragmenting of the ego; the ego works in the warmth organisation, in which a death process then takes place.

Rudolf Steiner pointed out that a partial death process in certain organs leads to different kinds of mental illness.[2] The function of the respective organ will then move out of the organic realm into the soul. For example, a death process in the heart will lead to mania. This can be observed in old people with heart disease. An old, tired and often immobile person with heart disease will suddenly become manic: he will jump up and throw chairs around or whatever happens to be at hand, and then sink back again into apathy. The heart contracts and expands, and when this occurs in the soul we encounter mania or its opposite.

Similarly, if a death process in the liver is transplanted into the psychological realm, we find depression and melancholia. A death process in one of the lungs will manifest itself in the soul as obsession, and in a kidney as hallucination.

Schizophrenia is none of these. It is a thought disorder — a split between ego and body. A person can live neither with himself nor with the world. It is a disassociation, a sliding out of reality, an inner contradiction. You will find this situation depicted in the film *Family Life* directed by Ken Loach and based on the work of R. D. Laing.

In 1956 G. Bateson,[3] when describing the schizophrenic condition, coined the phrase 'double bind', which is demonstrated by a typical example of an encounter between a schizophrenic patient and his visiting mother in the waiting room of a hospital. The mother stepped towards her son with a warm gesture as if she wanted to embrace him. The son, wanting to embrace his mother, approached her, but she let her arms fall and withdrew from him. He in turn withdrew from her. She again made a gesture towards him and again withdrew, and so on. This is a typical as well as harmful course to take with a schizophrenic person, but we do a similar thing every day: we go out to a person and then reject him, go out to him again and reject him, sometimes on a smaller, sometimes on a larger scale. We must learn not to do this. We must learn not to cause or enhance schizophrenic breakdowns in those around us.

We have no chance of preventing autism from developing, because we were not there at its onset. But we *are* present during adolescence when our youngsters go through the second stage of ego interiorisation. This second crisis can happen before our eyes, and sometimes we unwittingly contribute to breakdown situations.

I shall relate the case of a Down's syndrome woman, albeit no longer adolescent. After she had come to a new place, it was found that she was not only bullying her room mates but also telling stories of past adventures in Africa. Her fantasy certainly seemed to have taken over. It was felt necessary to 'deflate' her — to suppress the behaviour she exhibited to those around her, and to stop her storytelling. Her reaction to this was to make strange connections with her dead father, and she finally suffered a schizophrenic breakdown that necessitated hospitalisation.

Now this woman had found herself in a completely unaccustomed situation in the new place. Up until then she had been at home looking after her old mother. She felt the need to establish herself and preserve her identity. She attempted to do this, partly by her domineering behaviour towards her room mates, and partly by relating experiences she had actually had in Africa where she had spent her childhood. It was thought she needed 'deflating', but such a response can cause schizophrenia. It is our task to practise empathy: we must know what we are doing to someone else. We may be pushed into a situation where we feel like 'deflating' someone, but when we do so — and none of us is beyond such possibilities — we must realise it is our responsibility as a therapist not to do this.

* * * * *

To be a human being is one of the most impossible things there is. The older we are, the more we become used to it. But time and again we must come back to the existential problem. Whether as parents, teachers, therapists or whatever, we can only try every single day to be aware of the above two critical phases of childhood and youth. In the first of these we cannot help; in the second we can. The only way is to love, and to love with empathy. Love has no need to 'deflate'. Love is not always easy, but we must try and wrestle for every little step on the way towards greater understanding and for opportunities where we can help and not hinder our fellow human being.

Pre-psychosis and schizophrenia in adolescence

Youth Guidance Group, The Mount Community, Sussex, June 1985

Childhood psychosis: early years to puberty

Autism and early childhood psychosis are two separate conditions. We can regard them as polar opposites, and although a few symptoms may be manifest in both, nevertheless their fundamental character and outcome differ considerably. Autism may lead to considerable withdrawal from life and may be a prolonged condition. Childhood psychosis may in extreme conditions, if the youngster does not respond to therapeutic approaches during his early years, become overt schizophrenia during adolescence or early adulthood.

In other cases there may be little abnormality throughout the first 12 to 14 years before a schizoid tendency manifests itself. Detailed questioning of the family, and careful study of the school reports, will often reveal earlier warning signs. Parents may have proudly reported that developmental stages were exceptionally quick, and that their child may have excelled intellectually in comparison with his peers, but may have disliked physical exertion and games. Such a child's interests may have turned to technology while other children were still enjoying play. He may hardly have sought friendship, and although he may have been top of the class, he may have remained lonely, refusing to mix with his peers.

Such children should be observed with concern, so that necessary help can be given to them before a real breakdown occurs. Unfortunately they are often under pressure from parents and teachers to perform even better, to jump a class in order to take exams early and to specialise too soon, and this is especially the case with those who are exceptionally gifted in mathematics and physics. Their talent for music is often outstanding as far as technique and memory goes, but lacking in artistic sensitivity.

Physically, most of these youngsters shed their first teeth early, their growth in height is above average, and puberty makes itself felt precociously. They will gradually match the asthenic condition which Kretschmer* observed to be prevalent in the schizoid patient. Around puberty this latent disposition may turn into an overt schizoid if not schizophrenic state, although the later teens are the more usual time for such manifestations.

Schizoid tendencies: 14 years to adulthood

The impact of puberty on any child is a drastic one, but is usually met in a mood of adjustment to a new condition. Those who are predisposed to a breakdown will often succumb at this stage, particularly if there are other circumstances of stress, such as examinations, difficulties within the family, or parental expectations which burden the adolescent beyond his capacity. Within weeks, behaviour becomes more and more bizarre: obsessions begin to appear, fear in varying guises becomes apparent, sleep is severely disturbed, concentration dwindles rapidly, and any learning or practical application becomes impossible. Such youngsters may neglect their personal appearance and hygiene, lose the feeling of shame, and may seem to disappear into a different world of experience.

Their thoughts, full of anxieties and fraught with preoccupations, lose their logical basis and relation to circumstances. They may be inspired by voices or images which may assume compelling force. Eventually, in the more acute stages, such hallucinations will be acted out, often with sudden violence and without awareness of reality. Feelings are dulled and no longer attuned to their own thoughts, or with any consequences that may result from forceful actions. In these circumstances such youngsters are faced with a complete disruption of their personality, and it becomes justified to use the term schizophrenia, which derives from the Greek *schizo* — 'I split'.

---

* Ernst Kretschmer (1888–1964), one-time Professor of Psychiatry at the University of Tübingen, advanced the theory that certain mental disorders were more common in people of specific physical types. He posited three chief constitutional types: the tall, thin asthenic type, the muscular athletic type and the rotund pyknic type — the first two having a tendency towards a schizoid personality and the third towards a manic-depressive personality.

Three main forms of schizophrenia are observed depending on which aspect of the soul is prominent:

1 **Paranoia:** a hallucinatory form — the experience of being un-leashed, with unbalanced perception, while thinking remains uninfluenced by emotion or will.

2 **Hebephrenia:** a pathology that particularly affects the third seven-year period, in which uncontrolled emotions are in the foreground.

3 **Catatonia:** here will impulses are out of control — there can be an alternation between total inactivity, when such a patient may remain utterly motionless for days or weeks, and contrasting periods of extreme tension and restlessness leading to violent outbursts at the slightest provocation.

After months of acute disturbance, most patients with the above conditions might show some improvement. However, further relapses may occur in later years, each one leaving a definite trail of deterioration in the structure of the personality. Young people with these disturbances will need particular help if they are to master their lives, and only a few of them will later be able to carry out independent work under ordinary social conditions. Our task is to reach a deeper understanding of schizophrenia in order to be able to offer a way of life adequate to the individual's needs, possibilities and human dignity.

The illness has certainly been known for some time: the German poet Friedrich Hölderlin, King Ludwig II of Bavaria, the painter Vincent Van Gogh and the French poet Arthur Rimbaud all succumbed to it.[1] However, in recent decades a definite increase seems to be taking place. In the mid 1960s it afflicted an estimated 0.85 percent of the total pop-ulation. R. D. Laing in his *Politics of Experience*[2] put it at 1 percent. In our time, this pathology in its various forms has assumed a frightening preponderance in the life of many young people, posing the question as to whether this deviation of the human soul structure might have deeper spiritual implications, connected with the particular changes mankind has been undergoing in the 20th century.

Orthodox psychiatry has looked at the problem of etiology from many points of view. They may all have a grain of truth, but only a few go deep enough, such as R. D. Laing,[3] Victor Frankl,[4] Jean Foudraine [5] and K. Jaspers,[6, 7] who, through their interpretations, observations and sometimes their own experiences, try to pierce through the world of normal sensing to arrive at the 'threshold' between health and sanity. It is therefore highly relevant to include in the question of etiology consideration of the earlier stages of child development.

Birth to seven years

Throughout the first seven-year period, the model body (etheric) inherited from the parents has to be made one's own, as far as is individually possible. Until then the etheric forces devote their formative energies almost entirely to working on the organic structure, promoting growth and maturation.

This special interplay of physical and etheric bodies, with the first attempts at establishing the ego organisation, create the ideal conditions for imitation. Without the latter, the child's ability to learn to walk, talk or think would be severely hampered, and consecutive learning processes would not come about.

Precocious development

After the change of teeth a proportion of the ether forces free themselves from organic involvement and become available as soul capacities serving the process of remembering and thinking. In his first lecture on curative education,[8] Rudolf Steiner says that the forces which first build up our organs, especially the brain, metamorphose at the change of teeth into the capacity for thought and memory.

In children who are precocious in their intellectual development, especially those who are being overstimulated and pushed, the etheric body will free itself too early. It will then be available for premature learning at the cost of depriving the organs of sufficient ripening, and cause damage to the physical constitution for life. While intellectual precocity will be in the foreground for a time, the youngster may already show a marked emotional poverty as well as poor initiative. Initial interest in certain subjects may turn into obsessions and rigid preoccupations.

The modern craze to teach our children reading and writing at preschool age, and similar such bizarre ambitions, may lay the foundation for a later breakdown. Equally damaging is the habit of pushing young children through early examinations, or letting them specialise too soon in subjects such as mathematics and science, without allowing them to gain an all-round balanced and harmonising education.

Separation of the soul forces

One of the characteristic features in extreme cases of schizophrenia is the separation of the three soul forces.[9] Normally, thinking, feeling and willing present themselves as fairly co-ordinated faculties once childhood has passed. We have ideas and want to achieve certain aims, directing our will accordingly. Sadly, the schizophrenic patient will either lose or never achieve the capacity for directed ideation. When the three basic elements of the soul fall apart, this gives rise to chaotic, often bizarre or even dangerous situations, which are experienced by that person as well as by others. Actions may be totally divorced from their intentions and feelings may run riot.

A breakdown (by which we mean a breakdown in the harmony of the soul) manifests itself in diverse forms and degrees of derangement, but will eventually lead to the necessity for medical and/or therapeutic intervention.

Remedial therapy

Even in mild cases, formal educational studies should be reduced or avoided completely. Instead, a different life situation is called for, and a more therapeutic attitude will have to be adopted. It is important for pressure to be lifted as regards study or work, and to be replaced by a warm, tolerant and supportive environment. The ideal kinds of therapy will be artistic, ranging from music and eurythmy to the plastic arts and drama. Particularly helpful could be a period of curative eurythmy,* providing the patient is willing to co-operate. This treatment is helpful if certain organic defects can be diagnosed which have particularly affected the functional (etheric) element of an organ. Hydrotherapy and massage also have their place if the expertise is available.

---

* Eurythmy is an art of movement developed by Rudolf Steiner. Speech and music can be translated into movement through archetypal gestures expressed in an artistic way. Curative eurythmy is its therapeutic application. Insight into a particular condition can lead, under the supervision of a doctor, to the development of specific remedial exercises.

Therapeutic talks, especially in groups, can be useful, but the subjects chosen must be objective and not too personal or directed, aimed rather at dissolving one-sidedness and fixation in participants, and stimulating their interest in the world and compassion for the needs of others. Themes such as fear, responsibility, relationships etc. could be brought into the centre of a reciprocal conversation.[10] All measures should be accompanied by individual medical treatment.

Spiritual background

We can now return to addressing the question posed above earlier: why is schizophrenia an illness of our time?

From 1918 onwards, Rudolf Steiner noted repeatedly in his many lectures that mankind as a totality is in the process of crossing the threshold,[11, 12] and that although the age of the consciousness soul demands this development, we are mostly unaware that this is happening. We walk blindfold into the world of the spirit because our one-sided materialistic approach to life and culture prevents us from forming adequate concepts about spiritual truths.

In his book *How to Know Higher Worlds*,[13] Steiner speaks about experiences that we shall all have at the moment of death and afterwards. The initiate is prepared for this event during his life on earth, and will be able to meet the consequences of passing the threshold in full consciousness. Steiner describes in detail the severance of the three soul forces and the 'meeting with the Guardian of the Threshold', as well as the courage and spiritual strength which are needed to stand up to such experiences.

Some schizophrenic patients, and those suffering from other related illnesses, seem to have similar imaginations. This tells us that, beyond the threshold of today's normal sensory and conceptual way of experiencing ourselves and the world, there is another world which manifests in consistent forms, but which if encountered without preparation can lead to deeply disturbing and disorientating perceptions. An individual unprepared for these experiences, who has been brought up in our materialistic world, cannot embrace them without a severe challenge to his wellbeing in this life. As he passes the threshold unaware, the two worlds become totally mixed up. Spiritual images are seen as happenings of the here and now; earthly events are transposed into the other realm. For the individual living in this confusion, deeply rooted fears, emotions and unpredictable reactions may arise, and it is then easy to understand why violence, extreme bizarre behaviour and even suicide may occur.

In order to respond to the plight and suffering of such patients, and to become effective therapists, we need to familiarise ourselves with what spiritual science says about the threshold, and to take up the challenge of self-development and inner strengthening which is required. With this effort, allied to a serious approach to forming communities which express new social forms, such as those of the threefold social order* and the fundamental social law,† we can provide the kinds of environments which can offer help and healing for these distressing and prevalent conditions.

---

* Rudolf Steiner noted that the overall social organism can be described as having three main aspects — spiritual/cultural, political and economic — which he called the three-fold social order. We need to recognise these three, and the different approach required for each to function healthily.[14]

† The fundamental social law, described by Rudolf Steiner as early as 1905, can be expressed in the following way: if I work in order to meet the needs of my fellow human being, and if in turn others work also for the social good, then not only will each one's needs be met without the requirement for payment through labour being freely given, but the social organism itself will become healthy.[15]

Anorexia nervosa

Youth Guidance Group, The Mount Community, Sussex, June 1985

Though similar pathological pictures seem to have been described towards the end of the last century, the increase in the syndrome known as anorexia nervosa is certainly a special feature of our time. Anorexia appears mainly in girls at or around the age of puberty. Recent decades have produced many observations of symptoms and development, all of which unite to give a fairly characteristic picture that is comprehensible even for a lay person.

The girl may appear relatively unobtrusive throughout the first ten to twelve years of life, although to the experienced observer a more sensitive constitution may be apparent. There is no intellectual weakness — rather the opposite. Physically, a healthy appetite may even cause an increase in weight. However, a short time before the signs of puberty appear, the child refuses to eat normally, is preoccupied with her digestive processes, and may refuse to participate in regular meals. At other times secretive food intake may occur, which is soon thrown up again. As a result the weight may drop to a dangerously low level, which in extreme cases can be fatal.

Mentally, individuals affected will be bright, and will show a characteristic hyperactivity and restlessness. They keep others, as well as themselves, very busy, while at the same time exhibiting a rather rigid pattern, and a certain perfectionism in habits and activities. Should this lifestyle of precocious abilities and eating disorders continue for a longer time, features may become hardened and haggard, while the body reverts to the figure of a much younger child. This latter phenomenon alone could point towards the cause of this peculiar illness.

The moment pubertal changes manifest themselves in terms of bodily form and functions, such youngsters wish to refrain from becoming adults. Some may even express this by saying 'I don't want to grow up — I want to be a child again.' Others may be less open or conscious, but may nevertheless exhibit, in addition to the usual physical symptoms, a deep resistance to becoming older, to undergoing changes in their relationship to their parents and friends, to taking on responsibilities or greater independence.

Puberty is a hazardous watershed through which every young person has to pass. We are driven out of the paradise of childhood and begin to divine that we carry our destiny with us, leading us into an unknown future. Deep down in our soul, each of us has to summon up the will to decide to take up the challenge of living our life on the earth.

Once before, prior to conception, a similar challenge was put to us: did we wish to build up an earthly body and inhabit it with our full spirit–soul being? Not to take this step might result in childhood autism. Not to pass the next major threshold when growing up might bring about anorexia nervosa — a decision to remain in the sphere of permanent childhood and protection, which, however, cannot take place without leading to aberrations from normal development. A tendency towards such a resistance may be the consequence of experiences in a past life, but may also result from a difficult family constellation or an overpowering, demanding parent. Any of these may curb the person's willingness to take up life's challenge.

Inter-relationships within the family, and also within the peer group, will become more and more estranged. Such youngsters will become inwardly lonely, though outwardly even overactive, interfering and irritable. They will pursue their own wishes as to eating or fasting. They may adopt special absurd diets, or may be excessively preoccupied with their bodily processes. Their experience of the world around them will recede, to be replaced by an illusory picture of themselves and others. Their interests will narrow down to certain obsessions, combined with an ever-increasing egotism.

How can we help to heal this process of physical destruction, brought on by chronic starvation as well as the problems caused by human isolation and aberrations which can affect future personality development?

Rudolf Steiner called the event of puberty 'maturation towards the earth',[1] thus widening the popular conception that sexual development is its main feature. He makes us aware that it is the moment in time when, through the birth of the sentient (astral) body, the young person is turning his intellectual interest to the world around, and wakening up to his or her own emotional life as well as to the joys and sorrows of the world at large. In a healthy youngster, deep questions about life and its meaning arise in the soul. The physiological bodily changes are only a part of this general phenomenon.

In an anorexic condition, the individual loses her interest in others; learning may become sterile and automatic; questioning, should it arise, loses reality and only shows an egoistic trend. Any tendency to idealism might turn to unreality and illusion. In the bodily sphere, menstruation may cease or fail to happen at all, while all life processes decline dangerously and weight-loss continues.

Therapeutic approaches will need to be determined by the above description. First and foremost the loss of weight must be dealt with. Often only admission to a specialised hospital unit will achieve this, and the decision to take such a step should not be postponed too long.

Parallel to the physical care, a complex therapeutic programme has to be worked out, all with the aim of strengthening the will to live, awakening a broader interest in nature and human destinies, reverence for the suffering and struggles of others, and trying to open the soul to the true values, tasks and expectations of life. Involvement in the creative arts — music, eurythmy and curative eurythmy — may be necessary for years, as relapses are frequent, even after a long period.

Therapists, doctors and those closely involved in such cases need to show boundless patience, perseverance and humanity in order to carry the patient through the difficult phases of this illness.

We also have to ask ourselves why this syndrome affects so many young people today. Undoubtedly, the more vulnerable youngsters suffer from the deprivation of a fundamental support in their soul development as a result of our modern materialistic outlook on life, the increasingly precarious situations in families, and the lack of true and lasting values in the upbringing of children, be it at home or under the education system.

Of course, some of these comments can be seen as generalised views. However, there are many today who begin to perceive the effect life has on growing children and young people, knowing that a reform of our total lifestyle and educational values is needed if those who are passing through this receptive and also dependent phase of life are to gain the strength and harmony to pass harmoniously through the crucial period of adolescence.

Maladjustment and the human image

Glencraig Community, Northern Ireland, January 1979 *

We can observe that people whom we may describe as being malad-justed in their behaviour have not developed normal motivation. What might be the cause of this? It can be seen to go back to early in-fancy, when those responsible for creating the appropriate environment for the new soul rejected them, either before or after birth, and thereby failed to welcome them in an existential sense.

To try to understand this, let us try to conjure up the following picture. Before conception each human soul lives in a state of absorp-tion in the whole universe, and in the creative forces which weave around and work in us during this time. The descent through the planetary spheres, and the final pull, through conception and birth, into the confinement of the physical, is accompanied by the greatest anguish and terror. The care of the mother, and the heart-warming welcome of those who live around, are the only means by which the soul–spirit of the individual can enter without harm into the earthly and social environment of life. If the reception is unsatisfactory, then moral development will be impaired. Today this healthy reception of the in-carnating soul is denied to a horrifying degree.

How does morality arise in the human being? The small child is utterly dependent on the actions performed in its surroundings. Its mother and the environment belong to the bodily experience of the baby: all actions within the orbit of its experience become its own actions. Its existence in this situation is one of omnipotence. Yet present in the feeling of omnipotence is the anxiety that the care of those around may cease, that the child may be too much of a burden. A feeling of guilt pervades the young soul. This feeling of guilt calls for acts of

* Given at the New Year Assembly of the Camphill communities in Great Britain.

restitution. The small round hand lays itself on the mother's breast during suckling. These first attempts at restitution in a child are the beginnings of love. We can experience the continuous presence of a feeling of guilt as having been within us since early childhood, and the drive to restitution as the root of love.

Rudolf Steiner described two primary soul forces: [1]

- **sympathy** as the power of intentionality — hate, love, fighting, creating, etc. — all of these based on the blood

- **antipathy** as the attitude of reflection, cognition, consciousness, the possibility to be cool, withdrawn etc. — all of these based on the existence of our brain.*

We have to learn to mediate these two soul forces, and in the case of maladjustment to work especially on the ambivalence of sympathy.

In sympathy both love and hate are present at all times. There is no love without a tinge of hate, and no hate without intense interest. This omnipresence of hate in all our intentions causes feelings of guilt to rise, even in very early childhood. If this is not compensated for by deeds of restitution received from others, guilt can become the dominating content of the soul. If the soul is unable to cope with this predominance, the guilt feeling will lead to delinquent acts — attempts to justify the feeling of guilt.

We all know the experience of guilt with its ensuing conflict. It is the stimulus for the development of concern for what is good and evil — the power that will override all moral codes. Morality is not a natural faculty within human beings; it is fostered by human interaction from birth onwards, and this fact gives rise to so many of the complexities we experience in life. The quest for right moral perspectives is one of the essential features to do with the purpose of our life on earth.

Early deprivations, such as lack of care, the inability to gain restitution and to master the conflict existent with the emergence of guilt, cause damage to the motherly ether sheath into which we are wrapped at birth. The earlier this occurs, the more detrimental it will be for the development of morality in the individual.

---

* See also the footnote on sympathy and antipathy in the first chapter (page 20).

In everyone there lives, if only dimly, a consciousness of an image of what is means to be a human being. The bare physical existence of many people today is mostly abhorrent. Deprived individuals are much less able to cope with the discrepancy between their divine origin and the reality of their lives. What is needed is to receive such people into a situation which provides care in all aspects of human life. In such cases the usual pattern is that it works well at the beginning — the honeymoon period — but that after a time it becomes difficult. This can be seen as the delinquent period. In this latter period, the child or adult is attempting to reconcile his higher nature, which seems so unattainable, with his physical existence, and in this we have to assist him.

We can learn to utilise the three powers and gifts of the spirit which are there to be developed: faith, love and hope.

In the maladjusted person we meet:

- **mistrust,** which can be overcome by our faith in the divine origin of man, which gives security and help to the deprived person

- **hatred and lack of interest**, which can be overcome by our striving to love one another, by creating community and relieving loneliness

- **despair and despondency**, which can be overcome by the hope that eventually all our deeds will become meaningful, and fruitful for others.

In a nurturing and healthy family, faith, love and hope are there quite naturally for the child. Because these qualities are often severely lacking in the maladjusted person, they may have to be recreated within a later environment, such as a school or therapeutic community.

At school the classroom can become a sanctuary: here every day is new, yesterday's misdeeds are not carried over to today. The teacher is trusted and is upright. He can bring alive, not the supermen of today, devoid of morality, wreaking death and destruction, but the divine heroes who fought for and discovered morality in history. Science and nature studies should not be subjects of lifeless abstractions, but lessons that fill the soul with awe and wonder. Arts and crafts should replace the glaringly meaningless temptations of modernity, and help to build up self-esteem.

The Waldorf curriculum is an important guide for the maladjusted person, who is often so unable to distinguish between fantasy and fact. The subjects lead to the experience 'I identify myself with the world':

- in arts 'I express what I learn to find within me'

- in crafts 'I attain skill and educate my reasoning power'

- in work 'I form relationships in a team working for the benefit of others'

- in worship and festivals 'I experience the divine.'

A powerful tool for communicating with the sanctuary of the higher self is music therapy. Maladjusted youngsters are often musical and will handle an instrument with deep reverence. To create confidence the teacher lets the child play the instrument. Later he accompanies the playing with an ostinato, or lets the pupil play the ostinato and challenges him with a melody — major or minor, outgoing or inward-going. The youngster will learn a discipline which is not enforced but musical. Such seemingly simple exercises have tremendous depth and significance for someone whose soul and self-image is damaged, as it is for many maladjusted young people.

It is of real help to those who have been deprived of parental care to let them look after younger children or the less-fortunate ones in a house community or class.

The tendency to gang up and give way to an uncannily destructive spirit in a community has to be countered consciously by an acute awareness and the creation of a sociable and well-structured lifestyle. Delinquents will call up what is undisciplined in us and play on our emotions. In such situations we have to learn to be objective and act out of our egohood. In order to strengthen our egohood we can practise the *Rückschau*,* the eightfold path and other exercises.[2, 3] The maladjusted person will then come to recognise what we are trying to achieve and respect the effort.

---

* The *Rückschau* (a German word meaning 'looking back') is an exercise in self-development whereby the individual looks back on the events of the preceding day before going to sleep. This enables that individual to gain greater awareness of the actions and events of the day and thereby increase consciousness before entering the time of sleep.

On the many occasions when a maladjusted person creates disturbed human relationships through the negative side of the forces of sympathy, hate, aggression etc., we must rely upon our inner striving, as well as adding the power of antipathy. In talks and in our reactions, we can act as a reflecting mirror until the person can make sense of his actions for himself. As a teacher or friend we must avoid being idolised. The longing to find an idol in life should be guided into veneration for outstanding personalities in history through myths, sagas, tales and novels. Through the imitation of these mythical figures, life itself becomes meaningful for the deprived person. He discovers the meaning of his individuality and his identity. Therefore it is important that we understand him as an individual, not as part of a group. This understanding can be enhanced by discovering the events which led to the deprivation, and by leading him to a recognition and acceptance of the circumstances of his life.

In the social life of adults, maladjustment is difficult to bear and heal. It may be impossible without finding a relationship to the religious sacraments. As a mystical experience, these provide the first step towards attempts at healing. Even if these attempts eventually appear to lead to disappointment, the individual can experience that 'There has been a spell of time in my life during which I felt recognised and accepted as a human being.'

The more we can bring the holiness of human karma alive in our attempts to build communities, by relating our life stories, through communal activities, therapeutic talks and college meetings, the more will we be able to render help to the deprived person. We must cultivate an enthusiasm for one other, and the desire to give to each other what each one needs.

In all this, it is not only the maladjusted person who needs us as helpers; we ourselves develop equally by responding to the constant challenge posed by him. Just as Karl König and Thomas Weihs recognised the significance of the Down's syndrome child and the autistic human being,[4] so we can recognise the challenge presented by those we describe as maladjusted. We need to feel a sense of significance for what their behaviour is telling us, even if this is not easy to meet at times.

No other group faces us so forcibly with the social requirement for self-development, the necessity of finding the meaning of life within ourselves, and the need to form community life based on a true interest in one another, not on the adoption of roles and techniques. Thus what we term maladjustment or delinquency is a reflection of all that still has to be achieved in the family, social circumstances and cultural life of today. Such young people's suffering makes manifest its own cause, which lies outside them and which we, the so-called adjusted ones, have created.

Loving the stranger

Some thoughts on youth guidance and the inner path

Introduction

I have been occupied with a particular area of interest for quite a few years, namely with how our inner life can be formed so that we as adults can be more helpful to young people as they are going through the crucial period of adolescence. How we might do this will always remain an open question. This says something about the nature of the inner path and our having an inner life, in that the journey will be for ever unfinished, but always thought-provoking. This is because it is closely bound up with what is alive in us and gives meaning and impulse to our lives.

I will describe some experiences and events which have been relevant to my life and my questions. Aspects of what is conveyed may seem anecdotal, certainly non-academic, non-scientific, not conventionally psychological. You will, of course, draw your own conclusions, but I hope you will see that my experiences are linked to what I would call 'some answers' or 'some directions'.

In the summer of 1994 I was asked to contribute to the Youth Guidance Conference in Soltane, Pennsylvania, USA. The theme was to be 'Youth Guidance and the Inner Path'. The more I thought about this, even after years of reflection and study, the more difficult it became to find a starting point. Where was I to begin? Imagine this for yourself. You are approached on a particular subject because someone thinks you would be a good person to ask. They think 'He/she knows something about this issue.' But as the time to speak approaches, nothing has appeared to the one who is supposed to know. So for a while before my talk I remained at point zero: I had achieved nothing beyond having received the question.

While in this state of growing anxiety, I received a postcard from a friend of mine, Hubert Genz, who lives in France. It had a picture of a lavender field in Provence, and he wished me well for my journey to America and my talk. He also said that he thought one of Rudolf Steiner's lectures about karma, given in Breslau in June 1924,[1] might be relevant to the conference. At first I didn't react to this suggestion, but after a while I decided to read the lecture he had recommended. This enabled me to make a step forward. Out of the nothingness appeared the thread, and I grasped hold of it with gratitude. I mention this detail because it is characteristic of an imaginative, spiritual scientific approach rather than one based on natural scientific methodology.

The stranger

What follows is a condensed account of the main relevant parts of the above-mentioned lecture. I include a number of quotes because they present thoughts and descriptions of experiences which are essential in pursuing our question.

In his lecture Rudolf Steiner describes various essential aspects of child development which lead the individual to the threshold of puberty:

> Next comes the period immediately following puberty, the period between the onset of puberty and the twenty-first or twenty-second year. Just think of all that a human being reveals to us in this phase of his life! Even with our ordinary consciousness we see evidence of a complete change in his life, but it takes a crude form. We speak of the hobbledehoy years, of the 'awkward' years and this in itself indicates our awareness that a change is taking place. What is happening is that the inner being is now emerging more clearly. But if we can acquire sensitive perception of the first two life-periods, what emerges after puberty will appear as a 'second man', as a second man who becomes visible through the physical man standing there before us. And what expresses itself in the awkwardness, but also in very much that is admirable, appears like a second, cloud-like man within the physical man. It is important to detect this second, shadowy being, for questions on the subject are being asked on all sides today. But our civilisation gives no answer.

An understanding of what is happening, as described above, is not so readily available to the usual thinking of today. Whatever our understanding might be, however, it seems that it will arise from what emerges in the relationships people have with those older than themselves. Rudolf Steiner then turns directly to the nature of young people's experience of those who are older:

> There was this striving, this urgent insistent striving for an understanding of Man. Children and young people were ill at ease with their elders for they longed to hear from them something about Man, and these elders knew nothing. Modern civilisation can say nothing, knows nothing about the spirit of Man. But in earlier epochs people were able, speaking with real warmth of heart, to tell the young a great deal about Man. When thoughts were still quick with life, the old had a lot to say — but now they knew nothing. And so there was an urge to run, run no matter where, in order to learn something about Man. The young became wanderers, path-finders; they ran away from people who had nothing to tell them, seeking here, there and everywhere for something that could tell them something about Man.
>
> There you have the real origin of the Youth Movement of the twentieth century. What is this Youth Movement really seeking? It is seeking to find the reality of this second, cloud-like man who comes into evidence after puberty and who is actually there within the human being. The Youth Movement wants to be educated in a way that will enable it to apprehend this second man.

There you have the underlying, hardly visible, question which is clouded over and hidden by the attractive and seductive power of the Nike, Reebok, dance-music, designer drug, Budweiser culture.

> But who is this second man? What does he actually represent? What is it that emerges as it were from this human body in which we observe the gradual maturing of physiognomy and gesture, in connection with which we are also able to feel how, in the second period of life from the change of teeth to puberty, pre-earthly existence is coming to definite expression? *What is making its appearance here, like a stranger*? What is it that now comes forth when, after puberty, the human being begins to be conscious of his own freedom, when he turns to other individuals, seeking to form bonds with them out of an inner impulse which neither

he nor the others can explain but which underlies this very definite urge? Who is this second man? He is the being who lived in the earlier incarnation and is now making his way, like a shadow, into this present earthly life.

I would like to share two experiences regarding the appearance of the 'stranger'. The first occurred during a youth guidance conference at Soltane, USA, in 1994.

On our journey to America, my wife and I were joined by our teenage children, who were there for meals during the conference. We were sitting at a table having something to eat before the conference started. My son noticed his godmother walking down the path towards him: 'Ah, that's Penny!' he said. Not having met her for quite a while, he was delighted to see her. She walked up to where we were sitting and as we had been good friends for many years she greeted my wife and me and then sat down, ignoring my son. 'Hello Penny!' he said turning to her. It took a while before she realised who he was: 'Oh yes, hello Daniel!' There he was, her godson but, at the moment of meeting, a stranger.

A second instance occurred later. The family of a child whose son had been at school with Daniel was present at the performance of a Shakespeare play. Their other, younger son was acting in it and I recognised him even though I had not seen him for quite a few years, as he still had something childlike in his appearance. His older brother Nicholas, my son's ex-classmate, had left school a few years before. Daniel had gone camping many times with his family, who had maintained strong links, and he had sometimes visited our house.

During the interval, I was standing with our party outside the school building and could not help noticing a tall, thin young man. This was largely because of his appearance. He was dressed in black, with a long black leather coat, scraggy jet-black hair, studded belt, and so on. I don't know what the name for this is (if there is one) — 'punk', 'grunge' or 'gothic' perhaps? Still, I wondered, could this be Nicholas? After the play had finished and we were leaving, this black-clad youth appeared at the side of the path, turned to me and said 'Hello' in a really friendly way. It was nothing special, just a natural recognition of who I was. Just like Penny (see above), I had not changed my basic adult physiognomy, so I could still be recognised as Michael, in the same way that Penny could be recognised as who she was. But Nicholas, like Daniel previously,

Nicholas aged 7   *Nicholas aged 17* *

appeared as a stranger, as if they were both living examples of what was written on the page of the book I had begun to read.

As I was reading the lecture at the time, I enjoyed these moments immensely. Such situations arise for everyone who crosses over from childhood into youth. We all recognise the change even if we only make teasing remarks about the changing shape, the growing beard or the new nose. We cannot usually reach beyond these observations and the kind of fun we have with them at young people's expense. But we can go further than this basic level which recognises the presence of such a human phenomenon, whether it be in a girl or a boy. It can become our task to do this, because, as Rudolf Steiner says:

> From what breaks in upon human life *so mysteriously at about the age of puberty, mankind will gradually learn to take account of karma.* At the time of life when a human being becomes capable of propagating his kind, impulses to which he gave expression in earlier lives also make their appearance in him. But a great deal must happen in human hearts and feelings before there can be any clear recognition, any clear perception of what I have just been describing to you. [2]

We can begin to understand that, at the time when the second man or stranger emerges after puberty, there is present the person who lived before in earlier lives on earth. Therefore, my recognition of the

---

* Photographs reproduced by kind permission of Nicholas Koerber.

stranger's appearance is an opportunity for me to wake up to the reality of reincarnation as the core of what it means to be a human being on the earth. At such moments, when the reality of reincarnation is presented to us, we usually do not have 'the eyes to see or the ears to hear'.

Love

What follows may at first sight appear to be a puzzling change of direction as, following on from the above remarks, Rudolf Steiner starts to speak about self-love and selfless love and the way to recognise karma as it begins to reveal itself with the appearance of the stranger:

> Think of the great difference there is in the ordinary consciousness between self-love and love of others. People know well what self-love is, for every individual holds himself in high esteem — of that there is no doubt! Self-love is present even in those who imagine that they are entirely free from it. There are very few indeed — and a close investigation of karma would be called for in such cases — who would dream of saying that they have no self-love in them. Love of others is rather more difficult to fathom. Such love *may* of course be absolutely genuine, but it is very often coloured by an element of self-love. We may love another human being because he does something for us, because he is by our side; we love him for many reasons closely connected with self-love. Nevertheless there is such a thing as selfless love and it is within our reach. We can learn little by little to expel from love every vestige of self-interest, and then we come to know what it means to give ourselves to others in the true and real sense. It is from this self-giving, this giving of ourselves to others, this selfless love, that we can kindle the feeling that must arise if we are to glimpse earlier earthly lives.[3]

But what is the link between the development of selfless love and the stranger's appearance? Rudolf Steiner says that we have to imagine someone who lived a few hundred years ago, and another who lived even earlier. These two are both strangers, yet they are the same individuality, and in my own case will be present within me 'exactly as another person may be a stranger to you now.'

> You must be able to relate yourself to your preceding incarnation in the way you relate yourself now to some other human being; otherwise no inkling of the earlier incarnation is possible. Neither will you be able to

form an objective conception of what appears in a human being after puberty as a second, shadowy man.

But a way has to be found for this realisation to grow in an individual:

> Love that is truly selfless becomes a power of knowledge, and when love of self becomes so completely objective that a man can observe himself exactly as he observes other human beings, this is the means whereby a vista of earlier earthly lives will disclose itself — at first as a kind of dim inkling.

The first stage on the path we are trying to discover, and which is specific to the time of youth, leads to the recognition of the stranger. He begins to show himself at puberty, and indicates the emergence of a being who has lived before in previous lives on earth. This appearance is marked not only by the change in physiognomy and physique, but also by the change in the young person's emotional, intellectual and spiritual development. It is also present in the new focus of interest which that young person shows towards the world and others.

All of this process of becoming is part of a quest for self-recognition, which is linked to all the interesting and sometimes problematic aspects of adolescent development, especially in the area of family life. These phenomena are more or less the result of 'personal karma — own karma' coming into conflict or up against family, blood and other ties from which independence has to be sought. Our task is to try to understand what is taking place so that we can ease the necessary conflict, and so that it does not develop into warfare or other aberrations. This enables the healthy and necessary process of self-realisation to take place in the one who is gradually becoming a stranger and whom we have to get to know, make friends with, at the hand of the capacity for selfless love which we can strive to develop.

At this stage the reader is referred to Rudolf Steiner's lecture *The Human Heart*,[4] which, although it deals with matters beyond the precise scope of this chapter, provides the main focus for this book and the writers who have contributed to it. Suffice it to say that this lecture describes what takes place in and around the human heart at the time of puberty and its significance for the personal karma of the youngster. It is part of the indispensable source material for anyone who wishes to work with young people in a helpful way.

So far we have arrived at two important tasks:

- that of loving the stranger
- that of loving oneself.

This leads us on to the next part of the journey, which is already signposted in the final words of Steiner's Breslau lecture:

> But let us suppose that a thoroughly sincere member of the modern Youth Movement were to wake up one morning and for a quarter of an hour be vividly conscious of what he had experienced during sleep — and suppose we were to ask him during this quarter of an hour 'What is it that you are really seeking?' — he would answer: 'I am striving to apprehend the whole man, the being who has passed through many earthly lives. I am striving to know what it is within me that has come from earlier stages of existence. But you know nothing about it; you have nothing to tell me!'[5]

This means that to see the whole picture, to apprehend the whole man, we have to find a relationship with the world of sleep, as it is in the time of sleep, during this period of life, that the *whole man* becomes perceptible. Ordinarily we know little of what transpires during our sleep, but by accepting the help that anthroposophy offers us we may be able to learn something which can live in us as the source of further insight.

I recognise the stranger. Then, through what is realised by my effort to move beyond self-love towards selfless love, I may be able to sense that in this stranger, this new person, there lives someone who has lived before, who has had previous lives on earth, and who is the 'becoming' personality I now have to get to know.

What happens when we go to sleep?

A study of sleep is now necessary because our aim, as helpers of those who are in their time of youth, is to be of assistance to them in their search for meaning and direction, in the unfolding of their karma. We cannot apprehend the whole man, and in our context the young person, without relating to the wholeness of our lives and theirs. This requires us to bring our daytime, waking life in contact with what can be understood and experienced from our life of sleep.

If it is a clearer presence of individual karma which starts to make its appearance as adolescence sets in, this does not mean that there is no remnant of karma remaining from the time of childhood. It is only that after puberty the personal aspect enters more strongly and unites forcefully with the life of young people. They become themselves in a fuller way. This event is preliminary to what takes place later and which Julian Sleigh has called 'the birth of the ego'.[6]

It is this approaching presence of the ego which gives rise to the tension inherent within adolescence — the tension between the growing capacity for self-awareness and the dilemma of not yet being able to stand firmly within the sea of experiences which the new self-consciousness is throwing up during this time. Julian Sleigh provides a fuller description of what is experienced during adolescence.[7]

Rudolf Steiner, in a lecture on man's life in sleep and after death,[8] gives a wonderful description of what takes place during sleep. In this lecture he describes our experiences during sleep as being made possible in four different ways through the presence of the organs of:

- the heart-eye
- the sun-eye
- the eye of the whole human being
- what happens through the influence of the moon, which draws us back into our waking life each morning.

Given that this is an anthroposophical study, it is assumed that the reader has available some basic concepts relating to the nature of sleeping and waking, such as those described by Rudolf Steiner in *Theosophy*[9] or *Occult Science: An Outline.*[10]

In the above lecture[11] Steiner describes how, on going to sleep, a part of the astral body separates from the physical and etheric bodies so that it gains the capability of becoming perceptive towards the world which now appears to it and which is basically an 'out-of-the-body' world.

These perceptions happen firstly through what Steiner calls the organ of the 'heart-eye'. The heart-eye perceives what continues to move within the sleeping form lying on the bed and the effect the movements of the planets have on the still sleeping person. At the same time this perceptive experience takes place outside the physical body, and because of this it gives rise to the anxiety that this changed relationship to the body might continue and the connection to it be lost. This anxiety is enhanced by what Steiner describes as the gradual immersion into an unclear world which he terms the 'mist of the worlds'. This anxiety can only be overcome if the human being has already acquired in life a quality which is akin to devotion to the Divine. Instead of being overwhelmed by anxiety, I have to be able to 'give myself up to the Divine, to allow myself to rest in the Godhead.'

A second phase of experience arises through the organ of the 'sun-eye', which is linked to the solar plexus and the limbs. It is the zodiac which we now experience and we feel ourselves to be out there amongst the stars, feeling the forces which weave between them. Again we are filled with the anxiety that we might lose ourselves out there in the wonderful experience of the moving stars. According to Steiner, the anxiety present at this stage must lead over to an experience of inner harmony. If, in addition to devotion to the Divine, we have come to know the Christ as the being who passed through the mystery of Golgotha, for the sake of the earth and the universe as well as for the human being, then we will know that death does not lead to an end of life but to renewal and resurrection. If we possess this inner certainty regarding the forces of resurrection which are present alongside those of death, then the Christ can be our guide through the zodiacal starry world which we experience at this stage during sleep.

Now we come to the third experience. It relates not only to the heart and middle but to the totality of the human form, to the perceptive organ of the whole human being. Here we find ourselves within the living interplay of planets, zodiac and stars, and at this point we encounter our karma. It is the karma which has to do with relationships — with what happens between ourselves and others.

Here again Christ can be our guide and helper, as the danger here is that we continue our journey out beyond the zodiac and so die out of our earthly life. It is the moon's influence which calls us back, not allowing us, as yet, to separate ourselves from our earthly karma and the connection to our body. It leads us back towards the earth and we are drawn into our waking life, having glimpsed our karma and destiny.

These processes are ongoing and continue through the alternation of sleeping and waking as long as our karma directs us to live on earth. We can say that every night when we are asleep we learn something new about the working of our karma. We can do this because we see it and recognise it again each night through the perceptive eyes of our heart and limbs and our whole being. It has to do with what happens between people as well as with the nature of our relationship to the earth. Through these experiences the mystery of the Divine, of karma, unfolds within and around each and every one of us, daily and nightly.

One reaction to the above may be to say 'This is completely bizarre — heart-eye, the planets, mist of the worlds, solar plexus, the zodiac and all that. It's completely beyond me. I can't think about it in any reasonable way. So what's the point?'

No doubt, it is rare for people today to think about such things. We walk about in the world, and the reality of the footpath, the trees, the cars — all we see and hear — truly convinces us that this is the real world. Our main concerns are about what goes on within this tangible milieu. Everything else is somehow obscure and unthinkable by comparison.

On the other hand, we can create a space of interest within ourselves by recognising that we have unanswered questions about certain phenomena connected with our lives and the lives of young people. Drawing on the thoughts presented to us by Rudolf Steiner, we can begin to create a stream of ideas alongside our day-to-day practical world, which allows us to search for answers in relation to the idea of the whole person — this whole person having to do with the outer physical world as well as with an inner, generally non-visible world, and thereby with the combined worlds encountered during sleeping and waking.

What we have been concerned with so far can be described in the form of simple steps. Firstly, we recognise a new quality of individuality which makes its entrance at puberty. We realise it has to do with the personal karma of that individual in that something more of the whole person — who they are — is present, and thereby visible and audible to us. We will be able to relate to more of this whole person if we can develop a greater capacity for selfless love. Whether or not we achieve this is a matter for our own determination.

At this point we find ourselves thinking about this new presence as deriving from a world beyond that which otherwise and obviously belongs to the known hereditary–engendered reality. It is from another world — one which is difficult to describe but clearly has visible and real effects. This so-called other world of reality, which complements and extends the outer visible world, is accessible to us each night during sleep. This is what is described in anthroposophy — not an alternative world but the wholeness of the world reality. We can hardly imagine it or see it with today's ordinary eyes but it is nonetheless approachable through our thinking.

We have experiences and because we find them interesting we start to ask questions. If we have goodwill and are open to different ideas, then it is not a matter of believing one or the other theory but of searching for the truth, working with certain possibilities — theses.

Meditative life and practical life

Assuming that the reader has been able to follow the thread so far, we can now take a further step. Ordinary life, insofar as it relates us to earthly affairs — learning, working and meeting people — can provide us with a secure ground to stand on, psychologically speaking. But this ground can be shaken if we become insecure because of changes affecting our consciousness, particularly if they are of a pathological nature. Beyond this simplistic and inadequate way of describing the stability of our ordinary life, there is the subtle and varied world of what I might call my personal inner life, which I relate to as 'myself'. We move from generalisations, applicable to everyone, to the world of experiences which are solely mine.

We have all sorts of words to describe the condition of this inner world of experience — for example, peace, equanimity, love, anxiety, fear and so on — also, what we call goodness or the propensity towards evil. You know something about yourself if you ask yourself whether you are at peace, or whether you are a worrier, or someone who has to keep everything in his life under strict control. You can ask yourself if you are someone who makes himself available for contact with others, wants to create a space for meeting people, wants to have relationships, on all sorts of levels. Or are you just the opposite — shy, reclusive, nervous in the company of others?

Such thoughts about yourself can tend to float around as conjectures — partial ideas about what it means to be yourself. But you can also decide to change something about yourself which you don't like, or to try to achieve a measure of the selfless love referred to above.

You can also attempt to achieve in some measure the three goals of:

- acquiring devotion
- finding a relationship to Christ
- experiencing the mission of the earth.

If these begin to live in you — in your inner self-generated space — then your relationship towards sleep might become very different. In fact, a bridge would begin to form between the sensory world and a world which is normally accessible to us only during sleep, and thus usually unknown to us except through the uncertain significance of dream experiences. But how can we build these bridges? Where is the starting point? Perhaps the initial response to this question is to consider what takes place in us with regard to these three goals, even as early as the time of childhood.

From childhood to youth

We can attempt to engender the quality of devotion in the small child by encouraging his or her encounter with nature and with the phenomena of the world. It can also be discovered in the home. It will be encouraged because the faculty of imitation will enable the child to pick up on how others move — the gestures and the attitudes shown by adults towards the smaller and greater details of life. By this means the child will live within a world permeated by practical devotion.

How is the child to find the Christ? This is an ongoing process and is certainly helped by what we ourselves have found in our relationship to the fundamental impulse of Christianity. It is present in us if we have been able to some degree to get beyond a solely materialistic view of the world — not by ignoring the world, as we have to live within it, but by extending the way we think about it. This means beginning to live with the awareness of the process of dying and becoming which is present even in our thinking. We may not be able to do this so easily, but we can also be patient and wait until we can. This kind of contemplative waiting creates the space whereby the Christ can dwell in us.

In addition to this way of attaining devotion through the way we meet the world and through the inner life of those we meet, a significant role is played by the kind of religious life we encounter as a child or young person, a good example being the kind found in the Rudolf

Steiner Waldorf Schools and the Christian Community. Uniquely, these bodies have different services for people of different ages: the Children's Service, the Youth Service and, for adults, the Festival of Offering. Next to our way of experiencing the earth and our fellow human being, and an appropriate religious life, there is perhaps nothing else of an educational nature so potent for generating devotion — a healthy relationship to Christ and also a genuine love for the earth, such as can be found in the Waldorf Curriculum as practised in the Steiner Schools.

To summarise, then, there are three goals to be sought:

- creating a devotional atmosphere
- finding a relationship to Christ
- gaining a love for the earth and all humanity.

These three can in themselves open the way for a natural feeling for the truth of karma and reincarnation to grow in the child.

At first these possibilities are given, made available to the child. This happens within a space which is created by parents, school and life itself. Yet it is not only a matter of forming an outer framework in which experiences can take place; there is also the inner aspect which can also become meditative. By 'meditative' is meant the growing awareness of an inner world of contemplative, searching thought life which starts to become as real to the individual as the so-called outer life. As trees live in the outer landscape, so thoughts and imaginations live in this inner world and can be changed, lived with, experienced by the modern person in the way Steiner describes in *Knowledge of Higher Worlds.*[12]

The kind of inner world which is at first subject to inherent personality, family, environmental, national and other influences, and which grows out of our childhood background, can now come under our own control. As our childhood draws to a close, we begin to 'sort ourselves out' as regards our attitudes and way of thinking. Once we have made a start with this, and it requires an effort of consistent will-activity to do it, then we will have begun to clear a space within ourselves where our deepest interests, questions and concerns can begin to live, and to be listened to and researched. All this is in a way represented by the figure of Parzival, including all his encounters, failures, moments of awe and moments of despair. Perceval, the French name for Parzival, is associated with the French words *percer* meaning 'to pierce', *percevoir* 'to perceive' and *persévérer* 'to persevere' — thus for the meditative, inner life it means to embark on an inner journey which also has to do with our karma. With this we make the transition from our childhood into our youth. Those involved with youth guidance have at first to be simply aware of this.

The forming of destiny in sleeping and waking

Potentially we have gained a great deal from the three steps we have made, based on these anthroposophical studies. They have led to some thoughts on:

- the idea of the stranger
- the change in the human heart at puberty
- the stages of perceiving our karma during sleep.

Now there is a further step which draws us into its orbit and which encapsulates what we could call a fourth basic foundation stone for youth guidance. It is discovered in a lecture given by Rudolf Steiner in Berne in 1923 under the title of *The Forming of Destiny in Sleeping and Waking*.[13] Here again experiences in sleep are related to our daily life, and also to the conduct of our life. Put simply, it has to do with our ways of speaking, acting and relating to others.

The following picture emerges based on the lecture. If our speech is permeated by idealism, then during sleep we will be able to make a relationship to those beings known as Archangels.* It is they who are the recipients of what is nourishing within human speech. If our speech carries an inner conviction of soul or, on the other hand, lacks idealism, the consequences will show during the night when we enter the world of sleep. If our speech possesses this positive quality, and can be received

---

* Christian mystics of the 6th century A.D. spoke of a threefold hierarchy comprising nine ranks of spiritual beings, all based on terms used in the Bible, each of which is active in a particular way alongside the sensory world. The third Hierarchy, which Rudolf Steiner describes as existing beyond normal human consciousness, is made up of the Angels, the Archangels and the less familiar Principalities, which Steiner calls the Archai (following the original Greek). The Angels relate to the human being as an individual (hence the idea of a guardian angel); the Archangels are concerned with larger groupings, such as peoples or nations (hence the idea of a patron saint); the Archai are involved with what we call 'ages' — phases in the development of human awareness which we sense as a shift in consciousness (as that from the Middle Ages into the Renaissance, for example).[14, 15]

by the Archangels, this will help us towards the kind of hearing which we need in life. We gain a better ear for the voice of conscience, which we need to be able to hear, especially at crucial moments.

We then move on to our active life — to all we do with our arms and legs, our hands and feet. From the way each one of us works and carries out our daily tasks, our actions will express certain abilities and disabilities, a mere basic functioning or an artistic creative approach. The life of the soul reveals itself in fascinating ways. We see this, for example, in the French or Italian person's gestures which are indicative of a folk character. The soul aspect of the people permeates and pervades the person right into the gestures, into the fingers and hands. But this is still to do with the world of speech. What we need to arrive at is the next step — the step into deeds and how they are carried out. It is the realm of work. If our actions are carried out with enthusiasm and with satisfaction for something well done, then we will be able to permeate our life with a renewing faculty of thinking. Rudolf Steiner says that in this area we make a relationship to the Archai. They become our helpers, helping us with our thinking.

In both these areas, in our speech and in our deeds, we reveal our basic approach to life, and we can hope that this might represent our love and interest for the world. Therefore we can say that three qualities need to be present in us when we are around young people, being aware, as we can be, of what takes place each night during sleep:

- idealism in our speech
- enthusiasm in our working and acting
- a genuine love and interest in the world.

The above presents only the bare bones of what Steiner presented in the lecture referred to above, but what a difference it would make if, in our mechanistic age, we could approach our communicating and skill training while also seeing in them ways of engendering certain abilities and attitudes which have to do with the devotional interest in, and love for, the world.

In the various attempts to form therapeutic communities, upper-school classes and craft training, the activities undertaken need to include a wider perspective. Their purpose, and the approach we have towards them, is not only expressed in a timetable of activities, but has also to do with their after-glow — their after-effect when the young person goes to sleep. For it is during this time that future abilities and future karma are being worked on and assisted by those beings who are not rooted as we are in earthly sensory reality, namely the Angels, the Archangels and the Archai. Anthroposophy is there to enable us to think about these things in non-mystical, practical ways. The daily timetable in the various forms of upper-school education should be constructed and based on these three fundamental attitudinal approaches:

- idealism — in speaking
- enthusiasm — in doing
- love and interest — for the world.

These complement in the outer educational field what can already be present in the adult as the inner attributes of:

- devotion
- finding a relationship to Christ
- gaining a love for the earth and all humanity.

Of course, we can only attempt to gain these attributes on the basis of a moral world conception. Today we are moving away from such moral perspectives, of whatever kind, and they cannot be assumed or taken for granted in any field of social or educational practice. The impact of the so-called post-modern stratagem has led to a situation where moral preferences are seen to be of value to the individual if they so choose, but otherwise are left to each one to decide from his or her own perspective. Therefore it is considered best to leave the moral perspective out of the picture. This keeps everyone at an uncomplicated level, which suits the market-forces idea beautifully. Everything else is seen as only arbitrary, subjective, while the fact of the reality of the tree and the car is seen to be so unassailable that in the workings of the outer world, the mechanistic, physical, functioning aspect is seen to provide the most reliable and solid ground for everyone's conceptual feet to walk on.

This may be fine for the adult, in an age of so-called freedom, but if the effect of such a world conception begins to live in the way of speaking, the motivation we have towards our work, or our understanding of the world, then this will eventually influence and affect children and young people. There will be consequences for their health and wellbeing, as well as for their way of relating socially and their future destiny.

However, we can choose to look at things differently and to include in our daytime thinking the experiences which we have in the night. Then we can create a curriculum, and encourage practical experiences in the course of an educational programme, on the basis of a wider conceptual framework. Our learning and communication, and the exercising of our will, can happen in ways that help young people to connect and awaken to what takes place during their sleep. In terms of social education, this can begin to answer the question we opened with — the challenge of the young person which states:

> I am striving to know what it is within me that comes from earlier stages
> of my live. But you know nothing about it. You have nothing to tell me.

If groups of educationalists would only ponder on these issues, and face the challenge present in their own ways of thinking, speaking and acting, and their effect on the situation of the young person, then they would find that the above is nothing more that a basis for a practical pedagogy. But it will remain 'in the sky and out of reach' if we do not try to consider how we might put it into practice. It would need to be witnessed in its positive influence on the social health of young people. It is the latter which suffers so much because of their elders' intransigence over their own poverty of idealism and thought so that life is drawn into such unbelievable emptiness.

Now that we have attempted to examine how a so-called inner life, an inner path, can be relevant for our outer practical activities, let us go on to the next step.

The heart of youth guidance

> Have you forgotten that when we were baptised into union with Christ Jesus we were baptised into his death? By baptism we were buried with him, and lay dead, in order that, as Christ was raised from the dead in the splendour of the Father, so also we might set our feet upon the new path of life.
>
> For if we have become incorporate with him in a death like his, we shall also be one with him in a resurrection like his. We know that the man we once were has been crucified with Christ, for the destruction of

the sinful self, so that we may no longer be the slaves of sin, since a dead
man is no longer answerable for his sin. But if we thus died with Christ,
we believe that we shall also come to life with him. [Romans 6: 3–8]

If we approach these words of St Paul in a reflective mood, we recognise
the fundamental impulse of Christianity, which is to want to relate to
life so that the presence of the forces of dying and becoming, which are
inherent within it, are accepted and lived with in all situations.

We can put ourselves into the situation which Paul presents in his
Letter to the Romans. It is a situation which includes dying, burial, lying
in death, resurrection and ascension. We are incorporated into these
elements, and Christ is born and can live in us in as far as we include
this situation in our life. We then have a chance to overcome and trans-
cend the sinful self, put more of it aside. Sin means those aspects of
ourselves, be they word, thought or deed, which we recognise as not
living up to our self-avowed ideals.

Now one problem the young person, the stranger, has after puberty
is that his personal karma begins to unite more closely with the part
which has so far been his childish self. With this appearance there is
not only the phenomenon of a new psychology, physiognomy and
character, but also the arrival of new karmic aspects relating to the
individual which do not relate so easily to the karma which called the
individual into life at conception and birth. It is this new element we are
talking about.

The young person has to learn to accept his changing life, the new
face in the mirror, the body with its adequacy and inadequacy, the gifts
and the limitations — in fact, who that person is. Finding out about
oneself will include sinning in smaller or greater measure — or in other
words the person's own ideals are not yet clearly recognised, while at the
same time the longing to be himself and act on his own behalf is so
strong that he is driven out into the world unguided by others, and
unguided by himself — flying without a map. It is a right of passage
which cannot be avoided, though some try to avoid it by being a 'stay-
at-home', remaining conventional. Mostly they dive headlong right into
it while partially blindfold. There are many possibilities.

There is one encounter which includes all the above aspects and
appears in the Gospel of St Mark:

> As he was starting out on a journey a stranger ran up, and, kneeling before him, asked, 'Good Master, what must I do to win eternal life?' Jesus said to him, 'Why do you call me good? No one is good except God alone. You know the commandments: "Do not murder; do not commit adultery; do not steal; do not give false evidence; do not defraud; honour your father and mother."' 'But Master', he replied, 'I have kept all these since I was a boy.' Jesus looked straight at him; his heart warmed to him, and he said, 'One thing you lack: go, sell everything you have, and give to the poor, and you will have riches in heaven; and come, follow me.' At these words his face fell and he went away with a heavy heart; for he was a man of great wealth. [Mark 10: 17–22]

It is no good trying to intellectualise these few words. They are heart words, spoken out of a deep longing for renewal. At first the stranger speaks out of his boyhood adherence to the Old Testament — the approach to a world of eternal laws encapsulated in the Ten Commandments. Christ shows him that in order to renew himself he will have to step beyond these laws and this will entail sacrifice, dying and renewal. We can wonder about the way Christ is described during this encounter. It says he 'looked straight at him' and his 'heart warmed to him'. In the King James version it says 'Jesus beholding him, loved him.'

It is a description of an encounter. The Gospels are full of such meetings. Here it is the meeting of the stranger, the youth, with Christ, the one who knows that the way to eternal life passes through the valley of death and resurrection. Rudolf Steiner [16] pointed out the connection between this youth, Lazarus, (see below) and the one who, after Christ's death and resurrection, became John, the 'disciple who the Lord loved'. [John 13: 23] It is interesting that in three of the Gospels, just before the encounter with the stranger is described,* a quite different gesture is presented in relation to the child. Matthew's Gospel says, for example:

> They brought children for him to lay his hands on them with prayer. The disciples rebuked them, but Jesus said to them: 'Let the children come to me; do not try to stop them; for the Kingdom of Heaven belongs to such as these.' And he laid his hands on the children, and went his way. [Matthew 19: 13–15]

---

* Matthew 19, Mark 10 and Luke 18

This is just what was described earlier — the child needing to be embraced by prayer and blessing. It is quite a different gesture from the encounter with the youth. The youth is sent on his way and it is the Christ who waits, holding him at a distance. The question for childhood remains: are we able to embrace the child so that he feels the presence of the Kingdom of Heaven? How do we bless children today? How do we lay our hands on them? How do we educate out of a mood of prayer, of love?

The raising of Lazarus

In the encounter with Christ there is first a question, then a process of perceiving, followed by one of warming and then pointing the way, and also a leaving of the other one free whilst remaining close in soul, with Christ remaining connected to the youth through his heart space. Later there is the death and resurrection, the appearance of the new self. Lazarus is re-born. As John he lives on within the tidal power of the warmth and love extended to him by Christ. See Rudolf Steiner's account of the Raising of Lazarus.[17]

When Christ comes to the grave of Lazarus, he is asked why he did not come earlier as Lazarus is already known to him. With hindsight we can see that the youth had to die, or at least had to separate from his physical body during these three days in which he lay buried in the earth. He had to experience being far away from the earth, to see himself, his life, his knowledge, his karma and what he wanted to get beyond. In this time we can see him looking back over his life, his encounters, through the oculars of the heart-eye, the sun-eye and the eye of his whole being. His eternal 'I' looks down on the enwrapped body in the grave — the physical body which in the three days started to lose its finer force of life — and close to the moment of final separation, Christ comes to him and calls his soul and spirit back into his earthly body. Lazarus appears renewed. Christ accompanies his eternal being during these three days, through the night of the soul, through dying and becoming. He did this as a spiritual deed but also made it into a deed for the earth — preparation for what was to happen later at Easter.

We have moved seemingly from an anthroposophical study into christology, both aspects presenting meditations on the heart. Thoughts unite with warmth of heart, and our goodwill and intentions become an impetus towards love — a love for the earth, a love for the spirit, a love for one another, a gradually more objective love for oneself.

Youth guidance

Personal karma may lead us frequently into proximity with young people — not in a 'pally' way, wearing their style of tee shirts and so on, but maybe encountering them more often than either children or older people. We may be parents, educators, craft trainers, social workers, friends or mentors.

A question my arise: 'What are we going to do about James or Amanda?' Maybe they are raging against life, their family or they seem lost — anything is possible. Perhaps you ask them 'How are you?' or 'What's up?' and they may say 'I don't know what's going on in my life.' It doesn't matter what the reply is — what does matter is that they start to live in you, become alive in your imagination and space of interest, your heart space, and that because of this interest they may be willing to listen to you. A connection is made which becomes like a thread.

For a long time you may think about them. Now and then you may find them appearing in your thoughts; you wonder about them and how they are. You may find that one day you suddenly know what to say to them, or you may decide not to say anything or you just have to wait. Later, eventually, it will become clear either to them or in conversation with you how their life questions can be answered, either verbally or perhaps by life itself, i.e. through the working of destiny.

It is a world which you enter through your heart because the stranger has appeared to you and become the young person, and their question is to do with their destiny, which may need the help, interest and maybe the guidance you can offer. This guidance and help needs you to know not only about outer needs and factors, but also about the night — about what happens during sleep. You enter a world of awareness and in it the needs of the young person can begin to live and resound. It is from here, from out of the night, that answers can also come, in obvious but also less obvious ways.

Perhaps you can find the link in all of this, see threads and connections, ways of relating Christianity to the young person and yourself so that they form a whole.

The Christian path of encounter

Maybe we can see a pathway emerging which relates to the way Christ walked his earthly path of dying and becoming on the way towards Easter and beyond:

> The Washing of the Feet
> The Scourging
> The Crown of Thorns
> The Crucifixion
> The Mystical Death
> Burial and Resurrection
> The Ascension

This path is inherent in the way of Christianity. It appears in the same way that the eightfold path crystallises out of the way of compassion founded by the Gautama Buddha. A sevenfold path becomes apparent, and instead of our attempting to gain release from our karma, we dive into it, live into it, in the hope of being transformed, of finding new life.

The gesture of the *Washing of the Feet* is one of making the other person more important than yourself. The *Scourging* is having to face up to your self-love, your vanity. This is painful because you begin to feel your inner longing to be hindered by your egotism — the confines of your physical constitutional self. Wearing the *Crown of Thorns* is a true imagination for the tremendous battle you have to face in order to attain new thinking, and at one point you find yourself face to face with the world as it is, as opposed to the world as it could become in the future. This can lead to a form of non-physical *Crucifixion* — being crucified on the cross of world suffering and world becoming. It means facing loneliness, rejection, the presence of illness and death, the suffering of peoples, and misunderstanding in the sense of today's thinking, without there being an alternative.

The falling away of ordinary judgements leads you into nothingness, into the condition of not knowing. This is the equivalent of experiencing the *Mystical Death*, and here you must wait as if in *Burial*, before the grave of *Resurrection* can awaken you to a new way of knowing and of perceiving — perceiving what now ascends before me (the *Ascension*), the new self of the other one, not becoming, but having become.

Perhaps this is also what happens when our interest turns towards the young person, whenever or wherever the stranger makes his appearance. Instead of feeling annoyance or frustration, our task is to learn to love the stranger, to deepen our interest beyond our reacting self, to be a helper, to be able to offer something, to be a person who can have something to say about the human being. But I must be willing to overcome my self-love, to become less interested in myself. Loving the stranger, and loving myself in its non-egoistic meaning, opens the way to new thinking about the forming of destiny in sleeping and waking.

These three first steps, which can take place separately but are linked together, flow and interweave together, leading from my initial worldly thinking to the potential for new judgements, even though they may be at odds with the views of the time I live in. And the potential for new judgements calling for a death of old thinking leads me into the condition of not knowing. This is surely the state we are often in with young people, accompanying their becoming without knowing the outcome.

We can help them to go through this condition of uncertainty and confusion, sometimes even despair, because we live with these experiences ourselves. And that is the key: to wait as Christ waited for Lazarus, the youth, to become. But we can only do this if the waiting is carried out with attentiveness, not vacantly. What is crucial is the presence of oneself, sensitively attuned to the journey of the other one.

This is what suddenly ascends to view. The stranger begins to show the world and himself who he is, not ascending into the heights, vanishing from sight, but ascending before his eyes and others' eyes, having crossed through the valley of the shadow of death, becoming the bearer of a self, with his own ego characteristics. He can now enter into adult life as a human being who senses himself to be relevant and of use to the world, having started to overcome the debilitating influence of anxiety and meaninglessness which pervades humanity today. This can be summed up as the Seven Stages of Transformation of Thinking and Perceiving in Youth Guidance:

The Washing of the Feet	❀	To love the stranger
The Scourging	❀	To love oneself
The Crown of Thorns	❀	To develop new thinking about the alternation of sleeping and waking
The Crucifixion	❀	To overcome ordinary judgements
The Mystical Death	❀	To know nothing
Burial and Resurrection	❀	To wait and be attentive
The Ascension	❀	To perceive the stranger anew

It is not a step-by-step process, as everything is present simultaneously. What can come out of this is a way to form new life forces and a faculty of love that is not there because of grace but because I will it to be there.

This kind of willing is linked to the wisdom of the Grail and is the way of Parzival, who has to ask his question again today as a modern person and develop self-engendered interest in his neighbour. Trevrezent, Parzival's uncle, embodies the impulse of youth guidance. Parzival shares his frailties with him — what he has created out of 'not knowing what he was doing'. The Christian path of suffering and renewal is opened to him through Trevrezent. In a moment of complete loss of self, Parzival becomes available for healing. At this point Trevrezent takes his sins, aspects of his destiny, and sets him free to continue his journey towards the Grail.

Then follows the terrifying encounter with Kundry, who had previously shown him the distortions of his inner self and revealed them before others. She now tells him he will become Lord of the Grail, and of the Seven Spheres from Moon to Saturn. First she reflects back to him all that is sinful, in need of redemption. Later she points to the planetary spheres, the conscious rulership over sleeping and waking life.

On the path of becoming, the way of sickness, sin and death, the cross of the earthly passions and frailties appears renewed in the sign of the Rose Cross, where the seven roses entwine the black cross. The force of love gives birth to new life.

To ponder on these things is a way of becoming a human being who can perhaps be the kind of elder who says something about Man which can be understood and appreciated by the young person, who in turn may find a question on his lips which otherwise might not have been asked.

From Mars to Mercury

We have arrived at the symbol of the Rose Cross. What does it signify? Says Rudolf Steiner:

> If we associate the wreath of roses with the dead, black, wooden cross, with what the plant leaves behind when it dies, then we have in the Rose Cross a symbol of man's victory of the higher, purified nature over the lower. In man, unlike the plant, the lower nature must be overcome. The red rose can be for us a symbol of the purified red blood. But the rest of the plant cannot be an emblem in this sense, for there we must picture that the sap and greenness of the plant have lignified. In the black wooden cross we have therefore the emblem of the vanquished lower nature, in the roses the emblem of the development of the higher nature. The Rose Cross is an emblem of man's development as it proceeds in the world. This is not an abstract concept but something that can be felt and experienced as actual development. The soul can glow with warmth at the picture of development presented in the symbol of the Rose Cross.[18]

Therefore it has to do with all that has been described in the thoughts expressed above on the inner path, because we have tried to

> …show that man can have mental pictures which do not correspond to any external reality.

Thus this symbol leads us on the quest for an inner path which has primarily to do with the purification of the soul, and in this sense belongs more to the early phase of adolescence, beginning with puberty. It symbolises the whole process which the young person, as well as the older person, has to undertake to gain mastery over newly appearing soul qualities.

However, there is another symbol which belongs here: that of the Staff of Mercury (*see Figure 8*). What does this signify?

> Day alternates with night, waking with sleeping. During the day we have a number of experiences; during the night, without our being conscious of it, forces are drawn from the spiritual world. Just as we have experiences in our conscious life, in the night we have experiences in the subconscious region of our being. If with the object of acquiring

knowledge we take stock of our inner life from time to time, we can certainly ask ourselves the question: What progress am I making? Has every experience during the day brought me a step forward?[19]

It has something to do with day and night, waking and sleeping — also with the ego and our development.

> The advance made by the ego can be indicated by a serpentine spiral. Two serpent forms, one light and one dark, wind around a vertical staff. The light curves represent the experiences of the day, the dark curves the forces working during the night. The vertical line indicates the advances made. Here, then, we have a different symbol representing the life of man.

There are now these two symbols:

> In the Rose Cross we have a symbol of man's development from his present stage to his purification; in the Staff of Mercury we have a symbol of man's development through the experiences of day and night and the advance made by the ego. [20]

So you can see that there is a relationship between these two symbols. The Rose Cross can relate to puberty and what comes afterwards, the Staff of Mercury to the twofold alternating process we go through daily and nightly, and which combine to encircle the ongoing advancement of the ego. It would be possible for us to imagine that these symbols are present at the two thresholds of adolescence — the Rose Cross at its beginning and the Staff of Mercury at its conclusion, with the birth of the ego. With this thought we have arrived at something new. The path we have travelled, with all its questions and possible answers, has led us

Rose Cross   Staff of Mercury

Figure 8

to two meditative symbols which can live in and nurture the life of the soul, being for a long time a source of wonder and inspiration.

The time we live in is strongly coloured by materialism, intellect-ualism and the power of individualisation. These are just those elements which assail the young person during adolescence. Each of them entails a meeting with a death process. Therefore the question becomes 'How can I find eternal life?' — not immortality in a mythoogical sense but a life with meaning. The young person often says truculently 'It's my life!' — which is true, in a sense. But will he get beyond this death in self, in individualisation, and reach the shore of the true ego? — not the world of selfish love but of selfless love, where you can love without needing to be loved in return.

The struggle for this is represented by the Rose Cross, symbolising the development of the consciousness soul. In order to help we can picture to ourselves the Staff of Mercury, the ancient symbol for healing which, in imitation of Christ, accompanies the young person on his journey, in his day-to-day encounters as well as in those which happen during the night. We can only do this gradually by remembering, time and again, that there are two curves, the light/daytime one and the dark/night one. Our ego development as an expression of will is not only expressed in daytime assertiveness but also in our devotion, our relationship to Christ and our love for the world, all these having an effect at night when we fall asleep.

In this sense, the figure of the stranger whom we have to learn to love, despite this or that appearance or mode of behaviour, belongs to our time. For the same search is going on in the world, to find a way beyond selfish interest and individualisation — the way of the Mars ego — towards a new experience of self which we can start to picture as the true ego, symbolised by the Staff of Mercury. It is the way from the 'I' to the 'beyond-I', from Mars to Mercury.

Our efforts to understand this can help to form an inner space. In this we cannot speak of successes, only of the searching effort to create a heart listening space. If we do this, make this effort, maybe young people will recognise 'Yes, it is possible to know something about the whole man.' Whether or not they will ask about this is, of course, another matter. But this uncertainty should not hinder us from pursuing the task which is there to be undertaken.

Notes and references

Note: GA refers to the number of a lecture within the *Gesamtausgabe* (Collected Works) of Rudolf Steiner.

Adolescence and the human heart

1 Rudolf Steiner. *The Human Heart.* Dornach, 26 May 1922. GA212. Mercury Press, 1985

2 Rudolf Steiner. *Karma of Vocation,* 1916. GA172. Anthroposophical Press, 1984

The human heart is not a pump

1 Novalis. *Fragments* (no. 200). Phanes Press (USA), 1989

2 Walter Holtzapfel. *The Human Organs: Their functional and psychological significance.* The Lanthorne Press, 1993

3 Rudolf Steiner. *The Human Heart.* Dornach, 26 May 1922. GA212. Mercury Press, 1985

4 Lothar Vogel. *Der dreigliedrige Mensch.* Philosophisch-Anthroposophischer Verlag am Goetheanum, 1992

5 Rudolf Steiner. Quoted in Walter Holtzapfel op. cit., p. 74

6 Walter Holtzapfel op. cit., p. 81

7 Rudolf Steiner. *The Human Heart.* op. cit.

8 A Persian legend. Quoted in Rudolf Steiner. *Guidance in Esoteric Training.* GA42/245. Rudolf Steiner Press, 1994

9 Rudolf Steiner. Quoted in Bernard Nesfield-Cookson. *Rudolf Steiner's vision of love, spiritual science and the logic of the heart.* The Aquarian Press, 1983

10 Hildegard Gerbert. *Education through Art.* Mercury Press, 1989

Youth guidance and empathy

1 R. D. Laing. *The Politics of Experience.* Penguin, 1967

2 Rudolf Steiner. *The Gospel of St Luke.* GA114. Rudolf Steiner Press, 1988

3 Rudolf Steiner. *The Spiritual Foundation of Morality.* GA155. Anthroposophic Press, 1995

4 Karl König. *The Camphill Movement.* Camphill Books, 1993

Empathy I

1 Rudolf Steiner. *Education for Special Needs* (formerly *Curative Education*). GA317. Rudolf Steiner Press, 1988

2 ibid.

3 Rudolf Steiner. *A Psychology of Body, Soul and Spirit* (formerly *The Wisdom of Man, of the Soul and of the Spirit: Anthroposophy, Psychosophy, Pneumatosophy*). GA115. Anthroposophic Press, 1999

4 Rudolf Steiner. *Education for Special Needs.* op. cit.

5 Rudolf Steiner. *The Foundations of Human Experience* (formerly *Study of Man*). GA293. Anthroposophic Press, 1996

6 Rudolf Steiner. *Education for Special Needs.* op. cit.

7 Author's paraphrase of St Paul's well-known verses in the New Testament: 1 Corinthians 13.

Empathy II

1 Rudolf Steiner. *The Foundations of Human Experience* (formerly *Study of Man*). GA293. Anthroposophic Press, 1996

2 Rudolf Steiner. *Education for Special Needs* (formerly *Curative Education*). GA317. Rudolf Steiner Press, 1988

3 Max Frisch. *Andorra*. Suhrkamp, 1962 (only available in German)

4 Max Frisch. *I am not Stiller* (*Stiller* trans. 1954). Methuen Books, 1998

5 Brian Keenan. *An Evil Cradling*. Vintage, 1993

6 Raymond A. Moody Jr. *Life after Life*. Bantam Books, 1975

Insights into mental disorders in adolescence

1 R. D. Laing. *The Divided Self*. Penguin, 1965

2 Rudolf Treichler. *Soulways*. Hawthorn Press, 1989 (Chapter 4, in particular p. 132 ff, provides an explanation of Rudolf Steiner's comments)

3 G. Bateson et al. 'Toward a theory of schizophrenia' in *Behavioural Science*, vol. 1, p. 251

Pre-psychosis and schizophrenia in adolescence

1 David Stafford Clark. *Psychiatry for Students*. Allen and Unwin, 1967

2 R.D. Laing. *The Politics of Experience*. Penguin, 1974

3 R. D. Laing. *The Divided Self*. Penguin, 1965

4 Victor Frankl. *Man's Search for Meaning*. Hodder and Stoughton, 1994

5 Jean Foudraine. *Not Made of Wood*. Quartell Books, 1974

6 K. Jaspers. *Philosophy of Existence*. University of Pennsylvania, 1971

7 K. Jaspers. *Reason and Existence*. Fordham University Press, 1997

8 Rudolf Steiner. *Education for Special Needs* (formerly *Curative Education*). GA317. Rudolf Steiner Press, 1988

9 Rudolf Steiner. *Knowledge of Higher Worlds: How is it attained?* GA10. Rudolf Steiner Press, 1993. (Also published as *How to Know Higher Worlds*. Anthroposophic Press, 1994)

10 F. W. Zeylmans van Emmichoven. *Anthroposophical Understanding of the Human Soul*. Anthroposophic Press, 1982

11 Rudolf Steiner. 'Introduction to the Threefold Social Order', 1 May 1919. GA192 (Unpublished typescript. Rudolf Steiner Library, London)

12 Rudolf Steiner. *The Problems of Our Time.* 12 September 1919. Rudolf Steiner Publishing Company/Anthroposophic Press, 1943

13 Rudolf Steiner. *Knowledge of Higher. Worlds* op. cit.

14 Rudolf *Steiner. Towards Social Renewal.* London, 1997

15 Rudolf Steiner. *Anthroposophy and Social Question.* 1905. Mercury Press, 1982

Anorexia nervosa

1 Rudolf Steiner. *Education for Adolescents.* Anthroposophic Press, 1996

Maladjustment and the human image

1 Rudolf Steiner. *Social and Antisocial Forces.* GA186. Mercury Press, 1982

2 Rudolf Steiner. *Guidance in Esoteric Training.* GA42/245. Rudolf Steiner Press, 1994

3 Rudolf Steiner. *The Foundations of Human Experience* (formerly *Study of Man*). GA293. Anthroposophic Press, 1996

4 Thomas J. Weihs. *Children in Need of Special Care.* Souvenir Press, 2000

Loving the stranger

1 Rudolf Steiner. Lecture in Breslau, 12 June 1924. GA239. In: *Karmic Relationships* Vol. 7. Rudolf Steiner Press, 1973

2 ibid.

3 ibid.

4 Rudolf Steiner. 'The Human Heart.' Dornach, 26 May 1922. ga212. Mercury Press, 1985

5 Rudolf Steiner. *Karmic Relationships* Vol. 7. op. cit.

6 Julian Sleigh. 'The Threshold of Adolescence' In: *Adolescence and its Significance for those with Special Needs.* Michael Luxford (ed.). Camphill Books, 1995

7 ibid.

8 Rudolf Steiner. 'Planetary Spheres and their Influence on Man's Life in Sleep and after Death'. 30 August 1922. GA214. In: *Planetary Spheres and their Influence on Man's Life on Earth and in Spiritual Worlds*. Rudolf Steiner Press, 1982

9 Rudolf Steiner. *Theosophy*. GA9. Anthroposophic Press, 1997

10 Rudolf Steiner. *Occult Science: An Outline*. GA13. Rudolf Steiner Press, 1979. (Also published as *An Outline of Esoteric Science*. Anthroposophic Press, 1997)

11 Rudolf Steiner. 'Planetary Spheres ...' op. cit.

12 Rudolf Steiner. *Knowledge of Higher Worlds: How is it attained?* GA10. Rudolf Steiner Press, 1993. (Also published as *How to Know Higher Worlds*. Anthroposophic Press, 1994)

13 Rudolf Steiner. 'The Forming of Destiny in Sleeping and Waking'. Berne, 6 April 1923. GA224. In: *Angels*: Selected lectures. Rudolf Steiner Press, 1996

14 Adam Bittleston. *Human Needs and Cosmic Answers*. Floris Books, 1993

15 Sergei O. Prokofieff. *The Twelve Holy Nights and the Spiritual Hierarchies*. Temple Lodge, 1993

16 Rudolf Steiner. 'The Raising of Lazarus' In: *Christianity as Mystical Fact*. GA8. Anthroposophic Press, 1997

17 ibid.

18 Rudolf Steiner. *Macrocosm and Microcosm*. GA119. Rudolf Steiner Press, 1985 (See lecture of 28 March 1910)

19 ibid.

20 ibid.

Further reading

Adolescence (general)

1 Group for the Advancement of Psychiatry. *Normal Adolescence: Its Dynamics and Impact.* Crosby Lockwood Staples, 1974/Charles Scribner, 1968

2 A. C. Harwood. *The Recovery of Man in Childhood.* Myrin Books, 1992

3 *An Interrupted Life: The Diary of Etty Hillesum, 1941–43.* Pocket Books, 1991

4 Michael Kerfoot & Alan Butler. *Childhood and Adolescence.* Macmillan, 1988

5 Bernard Lievegoed. *Phases of Childhood.* Floris Books, 1997

6 Julian Sleigh. *Thirteen to Nineteen: Discovering the Light.* Floris Books, 1989

7 Betty Staley. *Between Form and Freedom.* Hawthorne Press, 1988

8 'Upper Grades and High School'. Articles from 'Education as an Art'. In: *Bulletin of the Waldorf Schools of America.* Ruth Pusch (ed.) Mercury Press, 1993

Psychological problems in adolescence

9 Maureen Dunbar. *Catherine: The Story of a Young Girl with Anorexia Nervosa.* Penguin Books, 1987

10 Erik H. Erikson. *Identity: Youth and Crisis.* W. W. Norton, 1994

11 Michael Rutter & David Smith (eds.). *Psychosocial Disorders in Young People.* John Wiley, 1995

12 Ved Varma (ed.). *Troubles of Children and Adolescents.* Jessica Kingsley Publishers, 1997

13 Lorna Wing. T*he Autistic Spectrum.* Constable, 1998

14 Donna Williams. *Autism: An Inside-Out Approach.* Jessica Kingsley Publishers, 1996

Psychological disturbances: Selected lectures by Rudolf Steiner

Note: GA refers to the number of a lecture within the *Gesamtausgabe* (Collected Works) of Rudolf Steiner.

15 3 November 1910. In: *A Psychology of Body, Soul and Spirit.* GA111. Anthroposophic Press, 1999

16 26 August 1916. *The Riddle of Humanity.* GA170, Rudolf Steiner Press, 1990

17 2 July 1921. In: *Psychoanalysis and Spiritual Psychology* (collection of lectures from various sources). GA205. Anthroposophic Press, 1990

18 12–14 August 1921. 'The Ego as Experience of Consciousness'. GA206. Unpublished typescript in Rudolf Steiner Library, London

19 30 September–2 October 1921. *Cosmosophy.* Vol. 1. GA207. Anthroposophic Press, 1985

20 6 November 1921. In: *Cosmosophy.* Vol. 2. GA208. Completion Press, Gimpie, 1997

Empathy

Note: These books include extensive references on the theme of empathy

21 Baruch Luke Urieli. *Kaspar Hauser Speaks for Himself.* Camphill Books, 1993

22 Baruch Luke Urieli & Hans Müller-Wiedemann. *Learning to Experience the Etheric World.* Temple Lodge, 1998

The heart

23 Karl König. *Earth and Man.* Bio-Dynamic Literature, Rhode Island 1982

24 Karl König. *A Christmas Story.* Camphill Books, 1995

25 Paul Pearsall. *The Heart's Code.* Thorsons, 1998

26 Ehrenfried Pfeiffer. *Heart Lectures.* Mercury Press, 1982

27 Claire Sylvia. *A Change of Heart.* Warner Books, 1998